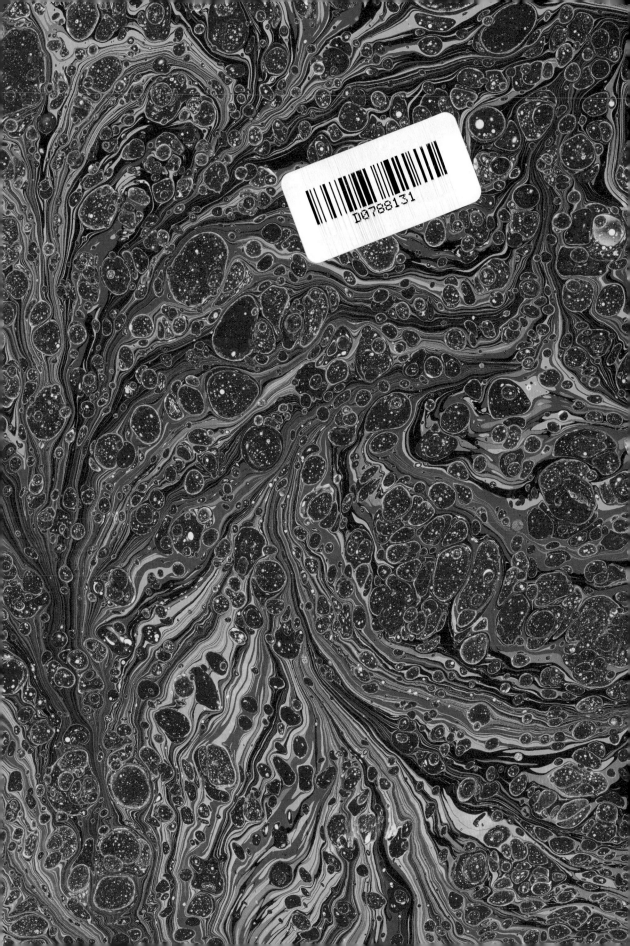

STUKAS OVER SPAIN

DIVE BOMBER AIRCRAFT AND UNITS OF THE LEGION CONDOR

STUKAS OVER SPAIN

DIVE BOMBER AIRCRAFT AND
UNITS OF THE LEGION CONDOR

Rafael A. Permuy - Lucas Molina

Schiffer Military History
Atglen, PA

Acknowledgments: The authors would like to thank the following people for their valuable help with the illustrations in this book: Raúl Arias Ramos, "Canario" Azaola Reyes, José Ramón Calparsoro Perot (†), José Manuel Campesino Bilbao, Miguel García Díaz, Heribert García i Esteller, David Gesalí Barrera, José Luis González Serrano, Juan Carlos Salgado Rodríguez and César O'Donnell Torroba.

Translation from the Spanish by Steve Turpin

This book was also published in Spanish under the title,
Stukas En España: Las Unidades de Bombardeo en Picado de la Legión Cóndor
by Galland Books, Valladolid, Spain.

Copyright © 2013 by Schiffer Publishing, Ltd.
Library of Congress Control Number: 2012955648

Printed in China.
ISBN: 978-0-7643-4368-1

We are interested in hearing from authors with book ideas on related topics.

Published by Schiffer Publishing Ltd.
4880 Lower Valley Road
Atglen, PA 19310
Phone: (610) 593-1777
FAX: (610) 593-2002
E-mail: Info@schifferbooks.com.
Visit our web site at: **www.schifferbooks.com**
Please write for a free catalog.
This book may be purchased from the publisher.
Try your bookstore first.

In Europe, Schiffer books are distributed by:
Bushwood Books
6 Marksbury Avenue
Kew Gardens
Surrey TW9 4JF, England
Phone: 44 (0) 20 8392-8585
FAX: 44 (0) 20 8392-9876
E-mail: Info@bushwoodbooks.co.uk.
Visit our website at: www.bushwoodbooks.co.uk

CONTENTS

INTRODUCTION

Anyone with even the remotest interest in the world of military aviation will have heard the word *"Stuka"* and will automatically associate it with one specific type of aircraft: the Junkers Ju 87.

The word *"Stuka"* however comes from the abbreviation of the German word *"Sturzkampfflugzeug,"* which literally means "dive-bombing aircraft." This is why the term is also used to refer to many other types of German aircraft, such as the Heinkel He 50, the Henschel Hs 123, the Arado Ar 81, the Blohm & Voss Ha 137, the Heinkel He 118, etc. But without a doubt the quintessential *Stuka* is the Junkers Ju 87.

In this book the authors take an in-depth look at the first operational use of the three types of German dive-bombers which served in the 1936-1939 Spanish Civil War: the Heinkel He 50, the Henschel Hs 123 *Angelito*, and the Junkers Ju 87 *"Stuka."*

After delving deep into Spanish and German archives, the authors believe they can now tell the complete story, down to the last detail, of the role played by the *Stukas* in the skies over Spain. We describe the operations flown by these aircraft in a succession of different units – VJ/88, *Stuka-Kette./J/88*, 5.J/88 and *Stuka/K.88* – from October 1936 to the end of the Spanish Civil War.

A major new contribution to the *Stuka* story was the discovery of Spanish documents which tell of the early operations, for a period of one month, of a prototype Junkers Ju 87V-4 *Stuka*, which was allocated Spanish code number 23-1; since it had always been thought that the only type-number allocated to this aircraft was 29. Another bonus for readers is the publication of illustrations of nearly every one of the twelve Ju 87V, A, and B types which served in Spain, since up until now inaccurate data has been published concerning the total number of *Stukas* sent to Spain. Another first is the inclusion of data stored in Spanish and German archives confirming the downing of a number of Ju 87Bs, either by enemy fighters or by hostile anti-aircraft fire, during the Catalonia campaign.

This work boasts the most important collection of photographs of the Heinkel He 50s, Henschel Hs 123s and Junkers Ju 87s in service in Spain. It is therefore our humble hope that readers will find this book to their satisfaction, a book which we believe sheds light on one of the most controversial issues of the Spanish Civil War: the combat debut of one of the most famous aircraft in history, the Junkers Ju 87 *Stuka*.

CHAPTER 1

The Arrival of the First *Stukas* in Spain

The supply of German materiel for the Spanish insurgents in July 1936 was conducted under the codename "Operation Magic Fire," for which purpose Special Staff "W" was set up. In early August the first shipments of six Heinkel He 51 fighters and twenty three-engined Junkers Ju 52s were arranged by the aforementioned Special Staff. Between August 28 and September 30 these were followed by the following shipments of military aviation materiel, as documented in pages 68 to 72 of the report entitled *"Das Unternehmen Feuerzauber,"* which is held at the German Military Archive at Freiburg:

Henschel Hs 123 biplane with three bladed propeller and civil German registration.

• 24 Heinkel He 51 fighters for the Nationalist Air Force.

• 12 Heinkel He 51 fighters to reinforce the German Eberhard fighter squadron.

• 3 prototype Messerschmitt Bf 109 monoplane fighters.

• 3 three-engined Junkers Ju 52s.

• 1 battery of Krupp 8.8 cm guns for DECA (anti-aircraft defense unit).

• 6,000 rounds for the above artillery pieces.

Bombs:

  • 12 x 250 kg bombs.

  • 120 x 250 kg bombs.

  • 1,000 x 50 kg bombs.

  • 200 x 10 kg bombs.

The aforementioned report, an essential document for our study, provides evidence of the shipping to Spain, for testing purposes, of the following aircraft:

  • 1 Heinkel He 50

  • 2 Henschel Hs 123 (*Stuka*), with aircrew and ground service crew.

Above: The first *Stukas* to arrive in Spain were two Henschel Hs 123s and a Heinkel He 50. They bore the codes 501, 502 and 503 respectively and were christened *Angelito* 1, 2 and 3.

Below: The Henschel Hs 123s arrived in Spain in the gray livery of the *Luftwaffe*.

In December 1936, the Hs 123 *Angelito* which still remained in Spain received the code number 24-1.

At the time these three aircraft were undergoing trials at the Rechlin *Erprobungsstelle* (experimental centre), because the *Luftwaffe* was looking for dive-bombers to equip its units specializing in this tactic.

So, in the second week of September of 1936 the German freighter "Wigbert" docked in Cadiz and offloaded two Henschel Hs 123s and one Heinkel He 50, probably all pre-series aircraft, which were immediately taken to the Tablada aerodrome near Seville for assembly.

The Henschel Hs 123, now with its camouflage paintwork, made its operational debut out of the Tablada aerodrome near Seville.

When these three aircraft arrived in Spain their upper surfaces were painted a uniform gray and their undersides were sky blue. Like all nationalist aircraft, a black cross of St. Andrew on a white background was painted on the tail, taking up the entire surface of the rudder. They were also adorned with black roundels on the upper and lower wing surfaces, with the same black circles on either side of the fuselage. During this early period, the two Henschel Hs 123s were given the military registration numbers 501 and 502 and their names, *Angelito* 1 and *Angelito* 2, were painted in black, also on the fuselage. As for the Heinkel He 50, this was registered as 503 and although we have no confirmation that it was given the name *Angelito* 3, it is very likely that it was.

11

Unfortunately there are no operational logs recording the activity of these aircraft out of Tablada in the months of September, October and November 1936. We only know that on October 6, 1936 these aircraft were still in Spain since on that day, for the first time, an instruction was issued whereby type-numbers were assigned to the various models of aircraft in service with the Nationalist Air Force. The He 50s were given the number 23 and the Hs 123s the number 24, corresponding to bombers. We also know that at least the He 50 and one of the Hs 123s were sent back to Rechlin and that the other *Angelito* remained in Spain, probably damaged during a test flight.

The Operational Debut of the Henschel Hs 123 *Angelito* in Spain

In November 1936 the German government decided to increase their participation in the Spanish Civil War and sent over the soon to be famous Legion Condor. Initially this air force unit did not have squadrons or flights of dive-bombers. However, there is information once again of the single Hs 123 *Angelito* operating in Spain in December 1936, thanks to the operations and aircraft movement logs of the Tablada (Seville) and Cordoba aerodromes.

The model of Hs 123 that operated in Spain had a metal, two-bladed propeller. Note the detail of the engine without its characteristic NACA cowling.

Around this time the Legion Condor organized an experimental unit in Seville, called VJ/88 (*Versuchsjagdstaffel*), formed by the prototypes sent to Spain: three Messerschmitt Bf 109 V fighters, one Heinkel He 112 V, one Junkers Ju 87V (to which we will be referring later) and, finally, one Henschel Hs 123, the latter two aircraft being dive-bombers. This unit was manned by German civil and military test pilots.

CHART I			
OPERATIONAL DEBUT OF HENSCHEL HS 123 (24-1) OUT OF TABLADA (SEVILLE)			
DECEMBER 1936			
AIRCRAFT	**DEPARTURE**	**ARRIVAL**	**ROUTE**
Dec 14, 1936 - Cordoba Aerodrome			
Hs 123	14:55 h	15:20 h	Seville - Cordoba
Hs 123	16:07 h		Cordoba - Seville
Dec 22, 1936 - Cordoba Aerodrome			
Henschel		10:45 h	Seville - Cordoba
Henschel	13:45 h Reconnaissance		Cordoba - Seville
Dec 23, 1936 - Information bulletin No.6. Seville.			
Movement and sorties: 10:27 h, Henschel, unnumbered, left on a special mission and returned at 16:20 h			
Cordoba Aerodrome			
Henschel	10:30 h	11:05 h	Seville - Cordoba Duration: 35 m
Henschel	14:45 h	15:45 h	Duration: 1h
Henschel	15:50 h		Cordoba - Seville
Dec 31, 1936 - Information bulletin No.14. Seville.			
Movement and sorties: 09:34 h No. 24-1 left for Cordoba, from where it made a bombing raid and returned to Seville at 15:47 h			
Cordoba Aerodrome			
Angelito 24-1. Pilot V. Zitzewitz.		10:20 h	Seville - Cordoba
Angelito 24-1. Pilot V. Zitzewitz.	13:08 h	14:05 h	Duration: 57 m
Angelito 24-1. Pilot V. Zitzewitz.	15:15 h		Cordoba - Seville

We know that on the 14th of that December the Henschel Hs 123 took off from Seville and landed at Cordoba at 15:20h, before leaving again at 16:07h, bound for the Andalusian capital. This aircraft was non-operational until the 22nd when it returned to Cordoba on a reconnaissance sortie over the Cordoba front before arriving back at Seville at 13:45h. According to Information Bulletin No.6 from Seville, on the following day the Henschel Hs 123, still without its type-number 24 painted on its fuselage, left on a special mission to Cordoba, from where it made a one-hour operational sortie before returning to Tablada at 15:50h.

It would not be until December 31 that bulletin No.14 from Tablada would record, at 09:34h, the take-off of the aircraft, now coded 24-1, with pilot V. Zitzewitz at the controls. The destination was Cordoba, from where it would fly a bombing mission over the front before returning to Seville at 15:47h.

Advertising poster featuring a Henschel Hs 123 with *Luftwaffe* markings.

The following month, on January 1, 2, and 4, 1937, the Hs 123 flew successive sorties over the Cordoba front, on what the Seville log called "special missions." We have two documents, both of which we believe to be hitherto unpublished and which we reproduce below, referring to German dive-bombers. These are dispatches Nos.88 and 91 which the Captain, Chief of Operations at Tablada sent to the "Chief of Dive-Bombers." The first of these, dated January 2, said the following:

"Given that there are no enemy vessels in the vicinity, it is my honor to bring to your attention two targets of great interest to our dive-bombers, which are the following:

Chart II
Operational debut of Henschel Hs 123 (24-1) out of Tablada (Seville)

January 1937

Aircraft	Departure	Arrival	Route
Jan 01, 1937 - Cordoba Aerodrome			
Angelito 24-1		13:15 h	Seville - Cordoba
Angelito 24-1	14:05 h		Cordoba - Seville
Jan 02, 1937 - Information bulletin No. 16. Seville.			
Movement and sorties: 10:10 h. 24-1 left for Cordoba on special mission and returned at 14:40 h			
Cordoba Aerodrome			
Angelito 24-1		10:42 h	Seville - Cordoba
Angelito 24-1	10:45 h	11:10 h	Duration: 25 m
Angelito 24-1	12:30 h	12:45 h	Duration: 15 m
Angelito 24-1	13:20 h		Cordoba-Seville
Jan 04, 1937 - Cordoba Aerodrome			
Information bulletin No.18. Seville.			
Movement and sorties: 10:20 h. 24-1 left for the Cordoba area and returned at 14:25 h			
Angelito 24-1		10:45 h	Seville - Cordoba
Angelito 24-1	12:45 h		Cordoba - Seville
Jan 06, 1937 - Information bulletin No. 20. Seville.			
Movement and sorties: 11:20 h 24-1 left for Malaga on special mission and returned at 14:25 h			

CHART II (CONTINUED)			
OPERATIONAL DEBUT OF HENSCHEL HS 123 24-1 OUT OF TABLADA (SEVILLE)			
JANUARY 1937			
AIRCRAFT	DEPARTURE	ARRIVAL	ROUTE
Jan 07, 1937 - Information bulletin No.21. Seville.			
Movement and sorties: 11:27h. 24-1 left on special mission and returned at 12:55 h. This aircraft was on a bombing mission against concentrations of trucks spotted to the north of San Pedro de Alcántara, the results of which were unknown.			
Jan 08, 1937 - Information bulletin No.22. Seville.			
Movement and sorties: 13:55 h. 24-1 left for Cordoba and returned at 16:35 h			
Cordoba Aerodrome			
Angelito 24-1		14:35 h	Seville - Cordoba
Angelito 24-1	15:15 h		Cordoba - Seville
Jan 10, 1937 - Information bulletin No.24. Seville.			
Movement and sorties: 13:18 h. 24-1 left for Cordoba and returned at 16:40 h Southern front. Out of Seville, a dive-bomber successfully bombed enemy positions on the Porcuna-Jaén line.			
Cordoba Aerodrome			
Angelito 24-1		13:50 h	Seville - Cordoba
Angelito 24-1	15:35 h		Cordoba - Seville
Jan 11, 1937 - Information bulletin No.25. Seville.			
Movement and sorties: 14:03 h. 24-1 left for Cordoba.			
Cordoba Aerodrome			
Angelito 24-1		14:35 h	Seville-Cordoba

CHART II (CONTINUED)			
OPERATIONAL DEBUT OF HENSCHEL HS 123 24-1 OUT OF TABLADA (SEVILLE)			
JANUARY 1937			
AIRCRAFT	DEPARTURE	ARRIVAL	ROUTE
Jan 12, 1937 Information bulletin No.26. Seville.			
Movement and sorties: 11:38 h. 24-1 arrived from Cordoba.			
Cordoba Aerodrome			
Angelito 24-1	07:45 h	08:40 h	Duration: 55 m
Angelito 24-1	10:20 h		Cordoba - Granada - Seville

1. *To cut the Madrid-Cordoba railway and road at Despeñaperros. This site is a gorge in the mountains between Santa Elena and Almuradiel where there are a number of tunnels and bridges.*

This railway is the only connection the enemy has between the central area and the south.

Impressive close-up of the engine of an *Angelito*. The pilot sitting on the wheel fairing is the Spanish *Teniente* Arístides García López.

2. *To cut the coastal road, if possible to the east of Motril, as it is the only supply route to Malaga. As the repair service is good, it would be advisable to repeat the sorties frequently.*

For the first mission Cordoba can be used as a base and for the second Granada."

The second dispatch, dated January 6, contains the order to postpone the second of the two missions:

"Further to my dispatch No.88, I am pleased to inform you that, according to instructions from the

Staff of the Second Division, the cutting of the road from Almería to Malaga should be postponed so as not to draw the enemy's attention to that area, and that you will be informed as to when you can do it at the appropriate time."

Nevertheless, on January 6 and 7, the Henschel Hs 123 24-1 flew sorties over the Malaga front in support of General Queipo de Llano's offensive. During the second of those days, the mission consisted of dive-bombing the concentrations of trucks reported to the north of San Pedro de Alcántara, although the log from Seville reveals that the results achieved by the Henschel were unknown.

Ground staff of the Legion Condor photographed in front of *Angelito* 24-2.

On the 8th the *Angelito* operated once again over the Cordoba front and two days later, on January 10, aircraft 24-1, flying out of the Cordoba aerodrome, successfully bombed enemy positions along the Porcuna-Jaén line. The Henschel Hs 123 operated out of Cordoba once again on the following two days but on January 12, the *Angelito* flew to the airfield at Armilla (Granada) before returning to Seville at 11:38h.

During the rest of January and the following February of 1937 the logs of the Seville, Cordoba and Granada aerodromes do not report any activity whatsoever of the Henschel Hs 123 number 24-1. It is very likely that the aircraft underwent a general overhaul at Tablada and, in any event, VJ/88 was disbanded shortly afterwards.

Stuka Kette 88 is Born

It was not until March 1937 that *Angelito* 24-1 was joined by another four aircraft, which were assembled in the Southern Region Air Force Depot workshops at Tablada. All of these aircraft were repainted in camouflage colors based on large angular patches of brown and dark green over the original gray, leaving the underside sky blue as before. They were given code numbers 24-2, 24-3, 24-4 and 24-5.

The five Henschel Hs 123 were organized into a dive-bombing flight (*Stuka Kette 88*) based at the Seville aerodrome. *Leutnant* Heinrich Brücker, nicknamed "Rubio" ("Blondie") in Spain, was appointed to lead the flight, aided by *Unteroffizier* pilots Emil Rückert and August Wilmsen. The Hs 123 of *Stuka Kette 88* bore the emblem of the flight, the so-called "*Teufelskopf*" or "Devil's Head," painted on both sides of the fuselage, just 30cm behind the engine cowling. According to British historian Gerald Howson, it is likely that the origin of this emblem was the deafening noise that their engines made at over 1,800 rpm, diving to attack enemy infantry columns and dropping their payload on the terrified troops. A truly "diabolical" effect.

It is more than likely that the first six Henschel to reach the Legion Condor included pre-series and series A-1 aircraft, although this is unconfirmed and practically impossible to know for certain, since the visual differences between them were minimal. As for personnel, *Stuka Kette 88* consisted of just fifteen people: three pilots, three mechanics, two armorers, one airframe specialist, one engine specialist, one supervisor, an interpreter and a driver, plus two civil specialists seconded from Henschel: Werner Busch and Walter Krone. To complete the aircrews of the *Kette*, these were joined by *Feldwebel* Fritz Hillmann (from 2.J/88) and *Unteroffizier* Hermann Beurer (from 1.J/88 and the pilot of the first Ju 87V-4 to arrive in Spain, in November 1936).

Note the detail of the "*Totenkopf*" (or skull and crossbones) painted on the fuselage. This was the personal emblem of the German pilot of aircraft 24-2.

According to Information Bulletin No.85 from Seville, on March 12, 1937, *Stuka Kette-88* made its operational debut. At 11:35h, aircraft 24-4 and 24-5 took off from Seville to fly a sortie in the Cordoba area but were forced to return due to bad weather at 12:25h. Two days later, on the 14th, the dive-bombing unit made two combat sorties. In the first of these, three aircraft operated over the area of Villanueva del Duque, where they bombed Alcaracejos due to not having seen any other target. The second sortie involved four aircraft, which reconnoitered the entire area, observing that the road from Hinojosa del Duque at the crossroads with the Peñarroya-Villanueva road was empty. On the Hinojosa to Villanueva road they saw between three and six trucks heading south. At the Cerro de Cabeza Mesada hill they spotted friendly signal panels. To the southwest of the hill and on the hill itself they saw a group of trucks and at Alcornocosilla there were more friendly signal panels. Between these hills and Villanueva they observed a fair amount of truck movement and the aircraft strafed two or three people at the level crossing between Villanueva and Alcaracejos. Also, to the west of Alcaracejos, close by the road, they spotted two artillery pieces. Around three kilometers to the west of Alcaracejos, in the direction of Pozoblanco, five enemy trucks were spotted. They successfully bombed Alcaracejos with a total of twenty-eight fifty-kilo bombs, but did not see any enemy troops or militia anywhere.

Illustration of German origin of two Henschel Hs 123s of the Legion Condor. Note the strange numbering and the triangular markings on the fuselage. This is a case of artistic license that has nothing to do with reality.

On the 15th, three Hs 123 aircraft flew a bombing sortie in the operational zone of the province of Cordoba, issuing the following report:

"Bombing of the town of Alcaracejos. Over and beyond the bridge over the river Cuzna. 4 or 5 trucks which were located to the east of Alcaracejos were machine-gunned and withdrew in the direction of Pozoblanco. The battery spotted yesterday was not seen today."

The following day two sorties were flown, the first with three aircraft in the area of Pozoblanco and the second in the same area with a pair of Hs 123s. These latter two aircraft, numbers 24-3 and 24-5, attacked the railway station of that town. During these operations, four of the aircraft were damaged; the German mechanics reported that they would take some time to repair.

However, on March 22 the five Henschel Hs 123s of the *Stuka Kette 88* were airworthy again, and at 10:50h they took off from Seville bound for the airfield at Almorox. After making a refueling stop at Caceres, they arrived at their destination airfield without event. For the first time *Oberleutnant* Brücker's unit was to operate over the Madrid front.

The following day, two Hs 123s accompanied the Heinkel He 51 fighters of 3.J/88 and made a low-level attack to the north of Titulcia, where they met heavy anti-aircraft fire and enemy fighters near Seseña.

On March 25 the first Henschel Hs 123 was lost in action. It was the aircraft piloted by *Uffz.* Konrad Rückert, which received a direct hit from Republican anti-aircraft fire during a brief operation over the Aravaca section of the Madrid front. The pilot had time to bail out and parachuted down into no-man's-land, where he was riddled with bullets fired by the Republican infantry.

The *Stuka Kette 88* operated over the Cordoba front and the Madrid front during February and March 1937.

According to the German dispatch, "*a squadron of Heinkel He 51s escorted four Henschel Hs 123 dive-bombers which attacked the Zarzuela Palace and enemy troops entrenched in some houses on the outskirts of*

Aravaca. During the bombing raid, and for reasons that are not known for certain, one of the dive-bombers went down in flames. The pilot bailed out, parachuting down between the lines. At the time of writing this dispatch, the impression is that the pilot was killed or taken prisoner."

On seeing the German pilot's descent from the nearby Nationalist lines, the Moroccan soldier, Aomar ben Abdelá, of the 6th Battalion of the Indigenous Regular Forces Group No.4 "Larache," tried, albeit unsuccessfully, to rescue the German, whom he supposed to be injured.

Despite heavy enemy fire, he reached the site of the wreckage of the downed aircraft and found the body of the German pilot. He later made an attempt to recover the body but his action was in vain, since the Republicans had beaten him to it. By Circular Order of July 3, 1937, ben Abdelá was awarded the *Cruz de Guerra* in recognition of his conduct during this action.

A Moroccan soldier of the 6th Battalion of the Indigenous Regular Forces tried – in vain – to rescue the German pilot *Uffz*. Konrad Rückert.

If we refer to Republican sources, specifically Information Bulletin No.25 of the Staff of the Central Army corresponding to the day of the event, we find the following report:

"... The enemy squadron which bombed El Pardo suffered the loss of two aircraft, one medium bomber and one fighter, hit by our anti-aircraft fire. One of them went down in flames over enemy lines, the former over ours. The pilot, of German nationality, bailed out and was machine-gunned by another aircraft of his own squadron, no doubt to prevent him from talking ..."

Rear view of the Hs 123 24-5.

The details and dates would seem to agree, but the cause of death of the German pilot put forward by the Republican dispatch is barely credible. We believe that it was more likely to be a justification of the actions of their own troops, rather than a plausible explanation of a somewhat unclear event.

The following day's Republican dispatch confirmed that the body of the German airman shot down the previous day had been recovered.

Above: The armorer fits two 50 kilo bombs under the wing of an *Angelito*.

Below: The Henschel Hs 123, number 24-3, was one of the aircraft lost in service in Spain.

The unit remained on the Madrid front until the end of March when it was transferred to Vitoria to take part in the offensive on Vizcaya. Unlike other German aviation authorities, the Chief of Staff of the Legion Condor, *Oberst* Wolfram *Freiherr* von Richthofen, had his own opinion about the deployment in combat of the Henschel Hs 123, and was more interested in trying them out in a close support and ground attack role (*Schlachtflugzeug*) – even though they had no radio equipment – rather than as true dive-bombers, a role for which von Richthofen did not consider them to be properly equipped. And time and practice proved this magnificent officer, cousin of the famous "Red Baron" of World War I, to be right. In the Poland offensive he went on to employ this same tactic, tried and tested in Spain.

CHART III
SORTIES OF THE HENSCHEL HS 123 "ANGELITOS" OF STUKA KETTE 88

MARCH 1937

Mar 12, 1937

Information bulletin No.85. Seville.

UNIT	MISSION
	Two aircraft left to make a sortie in the Cordoba area and had to turn back due to bad weather.
	MOVEMENT AND SORTIES
E-24	11.35 h. 4-24 left on a special mission, bound for Cordoba, together with 5-24, and both returned due to bad weather at 12.25 h **SOUTHERN FRONT:** The Henschel (two aircraft) left Seville to make a sortie in the Cordoba area, but had to turn back due to bad weather.

Mar 14, 1937

Information bulletin No.87. Seville.

UNIT	MISSION
E-24	First sortie, with three aircraft, against the Villanueva del Duque area, bombing Alcaracejos due to not having seen any other target. Second sortie, with four aircraft. They reconnoitered the entire area, finding the road from Hinojosa del Duque to the crossroads with the Peñarroya-Villanueva empty. On the Hinojosa to Villanueva road between 3 and 6 trucks heading south. On the Cerro de Cabeza Mesada hill they spotted our signal panels. To the S.W. of the hill and on the hill itself, a group of trucks. At Alcornocosilla our signal panels. Between these hills and Villanueva del Duque, a fair movement of trucks. They strafed two or three people at the level crossing between Villanueva and Alcaracejos. To the W. of Alcaracejos and close by the road, two artillery pieces. About three km to the W. of Alcaracejos towards Pozoblanco, 5 trucks. Bombed Alcaracejos with 28 x 50 kg in total, with great success. They did not see any troops or militia anywhere.

	MOVEMENT AND SORTIES
E-24	09:45 h. 24-3, 24-4 and 24-5 left on a special mission to Cordoba; the first returned at 11:12 h and the other two at 11:20 h 16:25 h. 24-2, 24-3, 24-4 and 24-5 left on a special mission to Cordoba and returned at 18:00 h **SOUTHERN FRONT:** The Henschel aircraft made two sorties, one with three aircraft and the other with four, in the Villanueva del Duque area, bombing Alcaracejo.

Mar 15, 1937

Information bulletin No.88. Seville.

UNIT	MISSION
E-24	Bombing raid with three aircraft, on the operations area of the province of Cordoba, with the following report: "Bombing of the town of Alcaracejos. Over and beyond the bridge over the river Cuzna. 4 or 5 trucks which were located to the east of Alcaracejos were machine-gunned and withdrew in the direction of Pozoblanco. The battery spotted yesterday was not seen today."
	MOVEMENT AND SORTIES
	15:35 h. 24-2, 24-3, 24-4 and 24-5 left on a special mission bound for Cordoba, returning at 17:20 h **SOUTHERN FRONT:** Three Henschels also bombed Alcaracejos.

CHART III (CONTINUED)
SORTIES OF THE HENSCHEL Hs 123 "ANGELITOS" OF STUKA KETTE 88

MARCH 1937

Mar 16, 1937

Information bulletin No.89. Seville.

UNIT	MISSION
	One sortie with three bombers in the area of Pozoblanco.
	One sortie with the same two aircraft as the previous one, reporting the following: "Bombing of the station at Pozoblanco, with great success. As they couldn't find the battery discovered the day before, they bombed some gun flashes coming from near the station, without knowing whether they were artillery pieces of anti-aircraft guns. The position of our column, which had left Alcaracejos, was some five km to the east of that town."

E-24	MOVEMENT AND SORTIES
	12:25 h. 24-2, 24-5 and 24-1 left for Cordoba; the latter returned at 14.00 h and the other two at 15:20 h
	15:50 h. 24-3 and 24-5 left for Cordoba, on a special mission, and returned at 17:20 h

AIRCRAFT	DEPARTURE	ARRIVAL	ROUTE
Henschel 24-1 Negrillo		12:55 h	Seville - Cordoba
Henschel 24-2 Negrillo		13:00 h	Seville - Cordoba
Henschel 24-5 Negrillo		13:00 h	Seville - Cordoba
Henschel 24-1 Negrillo		13:50 h	Cordoba - Seville
Henschel 24-2 Negrillo		14:10 h	Cordoba - Seville
Henschel 24-5 Negrillo		14:10 h	Cordoba - Seville

	CUADRO III (CONTINUED)
	SORTIES OF THE HENSCHEL HS 123 "ANGELITOS" OF STUKA KETTE 88

MARCH 1937

Mar 17, 1937

Information bulletin No.90. Seville.

UNIT	MISSION
E-24	No sorties were flown, due to four aircraft being damaged during yesterday's sorties. This damage will take some time to repair.

Mar 19, 1937

Information bulletin No.92. Seville.

E-24	No sorties, due to bad weather.

Mar 22, 1937

Information bulletin No.95. Seville.

UNIT	MISSION
E-24	Five aircraft left for Almorox, arriving at Caceres without incident.
	MOVEMENT AND SORTIES
	10:50 h. 24-1, 24-2, 24-3, 24-4 and 24-5 left for Almorox.

Mar 23, 1937

Legion Condor. I a

UNIT	MISSION
J/88	3 Squadron and two Hs 123 attacked to the north of Titulcia, flying very low. Heavy anti-aircraft fire near Seseña.

Condor Legion
Oberleutnant
Asmus

MARCH 1937	
Mar 25, 1937	
Legion Condor. I a	
UNIT	**MISSION**
J/88	*Tief angriff durch eine Staffel und vier Hs 123 auf Palacio de Zarzuela und unmliegende Gräben.* *Eine Hs 123 brennend abgeschossen. Pilot vermutlich in rote Gefangenschaft geraten.* Low level attack by one squadron and four Hs 123 against the Zarzuela Palace and nearby trenches. One Hs 123 shot down in flames. The pilot is suspected to have fallen into the hands of the reds.
	CENTRAL FRONT
J/88	One squadron of Heinkel fighters escorted a squadron of dive-bombers which bombed the Zarzuela Palace and houses on the outskirts of Aravaca. During the bombing raid, and for reasons that are not exactly known, one of the dive-bombers went down in flames. The pilot bailed out, ending up in no-man's land. At the time of writing this report the impression is that he was killed or taken prisoner.

The Henschel Hs 123 coded 24-3 was one of the aircraft lost during the campaign. The one in the photo is seen at the Tablada aerodrome (Seville).

As a result of painstaking research, we can say with absolute certainty that the date in question was May 22. We have found evidence proving that on that day a Nationalist Air Force Heinkel He 46, crewed by *Comandante* Carlos Martínez Vara de Rey and *Alférez* Valentín Izquierdo, was shot down over Ochandiano, both crew members being injured as a result. But on that same date another two aircraft of the Legion Condor were also hit by anti-aircraft fire: a Henschel Hs 123 *Angelito* and a Heinkel He 70 "Rayo." Everything seems to indicate that the Henschel Hs 123 managed to land, with damage, at the provisional airstrip at Ochandiano, as did the "Rayo." Both German aircraft had to be evacuated under enemy artillery fire that pounded the provisional airfield unopposed. The downed Henschel Hs 123 would never fly again and was written off.

Despite the loss of this aircraft, on May 25 the *Kette* of Hs 123s made – with its three surviving planes – three bombing raids on enemy field battery positions to the southeast of Yurre. On the following day the flight of Henschel Hs 123s dive-bombed some barracks two kilometers to the north of Orduña. After that date there was a pause in the sorties flown by *Stuka Kette 88*, which would not see action again until the start of operations to breach the "Iron Belt" in June.

Above: The *Stuka Kette 88*, then formed by three aircraft, lined up for inspection at their airfield.

Below: In April and May 1937 the *Angelitos* unit operated on the Vizcaya front out of the Vitoria aerodrome.

June 11 saw the third shooting down of a Henschel Hs 123 *Angelito* in a little over three months, over the eastern sector of the "Iron Belt" of Bilbao. The aircraft, piloted by *Uffz.* August Wilmsen, was shot down by the anti-aircraft artillery of the sector while carrying out a dive-bomb attack on the Basque fortifications. The Basque press at the time published several photographs of the wreckage of the aircraft and even of the German pilot who was killed in this action near Larrabezúa.

As an aside we should mention the publication of the news of the downed aircraft by a newspaper called *"La lucha de clases"* ("Class Struggle"), which focused its article not so much on the shooting down itself, but rather on the briefs the German pilot Wilmsen was wearing, making a crude mockery of *"such a feminine"* article of clothing, perhaps because in those days the only underpants seen in Spain reached below the knee. A somewhat grotesque anecdote in such tragic times.

A dispatch issued in Zamudio, on June 11, 1937, by the Administrative Officer of the 4th Expeditionary Brigade of Asturias, reported that:

Sequence of photos of the wreckage of the Hs 123 of the *Unteroffizier* Wilmsen, shot down by enemy anti-aircraft fire on June 11, 1937.

"... An enemy fighter came down in flames. I do not know whether it was shot down by our forces with rifle fire or whether it was shot down by enemy artillery fire. There are two versions. The aircraft crashed into our positions at Larrabezúa; the pilot was killed ..."

Above: An Hs 123 *Angelito* flies over a woody landscape typical of northern Spain.

Below: Headstone commemorating the German Hs 123 pilot August Wilmsen, which still exists today in the vicinity of Larrabezúa.

The official report from the Defense Minister for the Basque Country referred to the shooting down over the northern front (Vizcaya) of two three-engined rebel aircraft by enemy anti-aircraft fire, one of which, while obviously not a three-engined aircraft, must have been the aforementioned Henschel Hs 123. In fact, a dispatch from the Republican Air Force of the north sector Norte also claimed that two rebel aircraft had been shot down by anti-aircraft fire over the Vizcaya front, the only difference between the two reports being that the word "three-engined" had been removed and they were referred to simply as aircraft.

Meanwhile, by way of confirmation of the reports quoted above, for the first time we publish the report from the Legion Condor for that date, both in German and translated into English. The report mentions the shooting down of a second German aircraft, a Messerschmitt Bf 109:

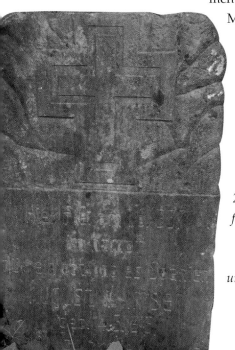

"Legion Condor.

J/88: Die Sturzbomber führten angriffe auf strassenpanzerwagen und strassenverkehr auf den von Larrabezúa nach norden führenden strassen durch.

Verluste: Eine Hs 123 ostwaerts Larrabezúa nach etwa 200 m sturzflug explodiert und abgestuerzt. Über flugzeugführer nichts bekannt.

Eine Bf 109 bei Eibar notgelandet. Flugzeugführer unverletzt. Über schaden an maschine nichts bekannt."

33

Translation:

"J/88: The dive-bombers made an attack on the armored vehicles and on traffic on the roads leading north of Larrabezúa.

Losses: One Hs 123 nose-dived for about 200 m before exploding and crashing east of Larrabezúa. Nothing is known of the fate of the pilot.

Above: An Hs 123 *Angelito* starts a take-off run on its way to a mission.

A Bf 109 made a forced landing near Eibar. The pilot was unhurt. The state of the aircraft is as yet unknown."

The two surviving Henschel Hs 123s, coded 23-4 and 23-5, did not operate over the northern front again and the *Stuka Kette* was disbanded. After both aircraft were overhauled at the Leon Air Force Depot workshops they were handed over to Spanish pilots who used them over the southern front. But that is another story that falls outside the scope of this book.

Below: Pair of Henschel Hs 123s in flight towards the combat zone.

The Republican Air Force and the *Angelitos*

What did the Republican Air Force know about their enemy's aircraft? We are assured that they were very well informed, or at least that is what the Staff of the Republican Air Force intended.

On August 10, 1938, the 2nd Section of the Staff of the Republican Air Force of the 4th Region published its Information Bulletin No.16 in which it referred to the "The Henschel He (sic) 123 single-seater fighter and dive-bomber." This bulletin includes three silhouettes of the *Angelito*, two retouched photographs, and an explanatory text of the most important features and performance figures of this aircraft. The information on this aircraft concluded with the following statement:

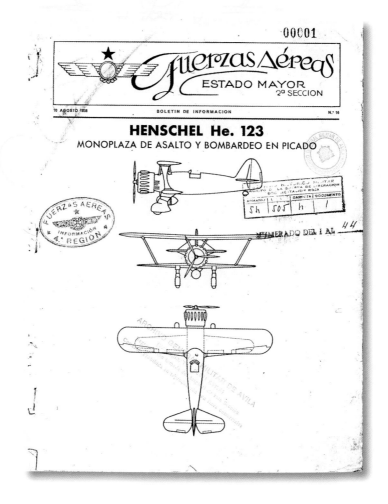

Information Bulletin of the Staff of the Republican Air Force concerning the Henschel Hs 123.

"... some of this type of aircraft used by the German invaders have been shot down by our planes."

While it is true that some of the aircraft used by the German "invaders" had been shot down, this had not been the work of the "Glorious Republican Aviation," but rather the effective work of the no less "glorious" anti-aircraft artillery.

In a special edition of this same publication, dated December 1938 and devoted entirely to silhouettes and features of enemy aircraft, the silhouette of the Hs 123 V1 was again published (this time with the mistake published in bulletin No.16, where its number was prefixed He, corrected), with the markings that these aircraft were thought to bear.

Una vista del Henschel 123 en posición de picado

Otra foto del Henschel 123 en la que se ve la robustez del montante único y los chaflanes de carenaje

Photos and text from the Information Bulletin of the 2nd Section of the Staff of the Republican Air Force.

00004

NÚM. 16 - HOJA I

MATERIAL ALEMAN

El Henschel He 123, cuyas siluetas y fotografías publicamos hoy, es un monomotor monoplaza de asalto y bombardeo en picado. Es biplano de envergadura desigual con un solo montante hacia los extremos. Las alas superiores rectangulares, con los extremos redondeados, y las inferiores idénticas y más finas. En las superiores lleva los alerones, y en las inferiores las luces de situación. El fuselaje es de tipo monocasco de sección oval. La estructura es metálica, y la envoltura también metálica, excepto en las partes móviles (timones, alerones, etc.) que van cubiertas de tela. El tren de aterrizaje es fijo, de patas independientes, cubiertas por un carenaje aerodinámico. Los amortiguadores por muelle anular «Uerdinger». Lleva freno en las ruedas, y la de cola es orientable. El depósito de gasolina está emplazado en el fuselaje detrás del tabique contra fuego, y los de aceite en el departamento del motor.

Lleva un motor radial en estrella de 9 cilindros B. M. W. 132, hélice metálica de paso variable que desarrolla una potencia de 550 c. v. Su armamento consiste en dos ametralladoras fijas y cuatro bombas de 50 kgs., colocadas éstas debajo de las alas.

Las características y performances son:

Envergadura superior	10'5 metros
» inferior	8 »
Longitud	8'6 »
Superficie	24'85 m²
Carga útil	660 kgs.
Velocidad máxima	355 km/h.
» mínima	100 »
Radio de acción	850 km.
Techo	8400 metros

De este tipo, que los invasores alemanes usan, ha sido derribado alguno por nuestros cazas.

But as nothing is perfect in this world, the drawings were captioned: "*... It seems that it is not yet used in Spain.*"

And the war was in its final stages!

The two surviving Hs 123s of the Legion Condor were handed over to Spanish pilots in the autumn of 1937. Before the Civil War ended the Nationalist Air Force made an order for twelve Hs 123 A-1s, now fitted with headrests as can be seen in both photos. The aircraft were received just after the Civil War ended.

To close this chapter, the Legion Condor's accounts reveal that, through this unit General Kindelán's Nationalist Air Force ordered another twelve Henschel Hs 123 aircraft, which were incorporated into the *Aviación Nacional* after the war had already ended and, together with the two already in service, formed the Dive-Bombing Squadron of the Southern Air Region under the command of *Comandante* Antonio Sanz García Veas.

CHAPTER 2

The Junkers Ju 87 *Stuka*

"It is not known what type of aircraft this is."

O n December 25, 1936, Christmas Day, Information Bulletin
No.8 from the Operations Section of the Tablada Military
Aerodrome (Seville), in its section on the movements and sorties of
the aircraft based there, included the following report, the content of
which is rather surprising:

*"At 12:35h the aircraft coded 23-1 took off on a special mission,
returning at 13:10h. It is not known what type of aircraft this is."*

In other words, the very officer responsible for the aerodrome's
information service, *Capitán* Fernando Medina Benjumea, had no idea
what type of aircraft was flying under that code number nor what
mission it was on.

The Junkers Ju 87
coded D-UBIP was the
prototype V-4 of this
aircraft. It was sent
secretly to Spain in
December 1936.

The mysterious aircraft coded 23-1 was the German prototype Junkers Ju 87V-4, a model which at the time was undergoing trials at the *Erprobungsstelle* (test center) at Rechlin, which was secretly sent over to Spain during December 1936 to be tested under operational conditions in the skies of Spain. The aircraft was attached to an experimental unit of the Legion Condor called VJ/88. This small test squadron contained the three prototype Messerschmitt Bf 109 fighters, one prototype Heinkel He 112 fighter, and another prototype Henschel Hs 123 dive-bomber. A Heinkel He 50 and another Hs 123 which had formed part of the unit had already been written off by this time.

Above: Once tried and tested in Spain, the Ju 87 *Stuka* went into series production for *Luftwaffe* units.

Below: Irrefutable evidence. A document from the Staff of the Nationalist Air Force in which type number 23 was assigned to the first Junkers Ju 87 *Stuka* operating in Spain, not type number 29.

The Germans tried so hard to keep the Junkers Ju 87 secret that they strictly prohibited the Spanish from getting near it or taking photographs of it. Nevertheless, according to the personal testimony of *General* Jesús Salas Larrazábal, towards the end of December a bold Spanish flier managed to take a photograph of it, at dusk and seen from behind, from a window of the Southern Region Air Force Depot workshops at Tablada. *General* Salas himself actually saw the photograph, saying that it was a little dark but the Ju 87 could be identified perfectly. Everything would seem to indicate that this snapshot has been lost, or else it is in private hands and has never been published. A pity.

According to German sources, the pilots entrusted to test the prototype Ju 87V-4 were *Unteroffizier* Hermann Beurer and the civil pilot V. Zitzewitz.

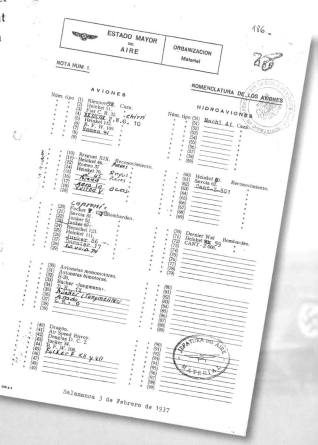

The former was initially assigned to fly one of the Messerschmitt Bf 109 prototypes, but a serious accident led to that aircraft being written off, while Zitzewitz alternated this task with test flights of the Henschel Hs 123 *Angelito* number 24-1, as we mentioned previously.

As was also mentioned earlier, in October 1936 type-number 23 was assigned to the Heinkel He 50. We know that this model returned to Rechlin immediately, whereupon, in December 1936, Air Command reassigned the vacant type-number to the recently arrived prototype Junkers Ju 87V-4.

The Operational Debut of the Junkers Ju 87V-4 in Spain

On December 27, at 10:40h, Junkers Ju 87 23-1 left Seville bound for Salamanca, very probably to put on a demonstration for the top brass of the Legion Condor, since at the time the Staff of the German air unit was based in Salamanca. The aircraft returned to Tablada at 16:00h the following day.

We should remember that at that time the future Chief of Staff of the Legion Condor, *Oberst* Wolfram von Richthofen, was the head of the test group of the Technical Office of the *Luftwaffe* in Berlin, among whose responsibilities was the monitoring of the development of the

Junkers Ju 87 and the Heinkel He 112 prototypes. Both aircraft were operating in Spain at the time and it is safe to assume that it was von Richthofen who took the decision to send them to the peninsula. A little later, January 20, 1937, to be precise, this high-ranking officer would take over from Major Alexander Holle as Chief of Staff of the Legion Condor, when the Ju 87V-4 had already returned to Germany.

Above: Detail of the bomb bay of a Ju 87 *Stuka*, where it could carry a 500 kilo bomb.

Below: Wolfram *von* Richthofen, who was Chief of Staff and the last leader of the Legion Condor, in 1936 led the Junkers Ju 87 test group in Germany.

It was not until December 31 that the Ju 87 number 23-1 made its first operational flight in Spain, on what the Tablada log called a "special mission." The aircraft took off at 09:34h, returning to the Seville aerodrome at 11:05h; in all likelihood it was in action over the Cordoba front, which was quite active around that time.

At 12:42h on New Year's Day, 1937, *Stuka* 23-1 took off to make another sortie over the Cordoba front and, on its completion, landed at the aerodrome at Cordoba at 13:20h. Shortly afterwards, having refueled, it left at 14:05h, bound for Seville, landing there at 15:27h.

On the morning of January 2, the new Junkers 23-1 dive-bomber, as the Cordoba aerodrome logs referred to it, made another ground attack sortie on that front, once again stopping to refuel at Cordoba aerodrome before returning to Seville.

Repeated sorties against the Cordoba front were made, in a similar manner to the attacks described above, on January 4, 5, 6, and 8 of 1937, and on the following day the official logs of Seville and Avila recorded the last flight in Spain of the V-4 prototype Junkers Ju 87. On that day, 23-1 left Tablada at 11:07h bound for Avila, where it landed without event before returning to the Seville aerodrome at 16:20h.

Above: A Junkers Ju 87A of the first series for the *Luftwaffe* still bearing a civil air registration number.

Below: Detail of an Information Bulletin of the Staff of the Republican Air Force with a photo of the prototype Ju 87V-4.

After that there is no further record of that *Stuka* operating in Spain. No doubt the aircraft was dismantled, crated, and sent by sea to Germany, where it successfully completed its trials and served as number one in the A-0 series of the Junkers Ju 87 that immediately went into production for the *Luftwaffe*.

CHART IV
SORTIES MADE BY THE FIRST JUNKERS JU 87V-4 *STUKA* (23-1) OUT OF THE AERODROMES OF TABLADA (SEVILLE) AND CORDOBA

DECEMBER 1936

DATE	BULLETIN	PLACE	MOVEMENT AND SORTIES
DEC 25, 1936	Information bulletin No.8	Seville	12:35 h. 23-1 left on a special mission, returning at 13:10 h. It is not known what type of airplane this is.
DEC 27, 1936	Information bulletin No.10	Seville	10:40 h. 23-1 left for Salamanca.
DEC 28, 1936	Information bulletin No.11	Seville	16.00 h. 23-1 arrived from Salamanca.
DEC 31, 1936	Information bulletin No.14	Seville	09:34 h. 23-1 left on a special mission, returning at 11 h 05 m.

JANUARY 1937

DATE	BULLETIN	PLACE	MOVEMENT AND SORTIES
JAN 01, 1937	Information bulletin No.15	Seville	12:42 h. 23-1 left for the same mission (bombing), returning without incident at 15:27 h Seville-Cordoba.
			Cordoba Aerodrome Junkers 23-1 dive-bomber. Arrival: 13:20 h Seville-Cordoba. Junkers 23-1 dive-bomber. Departure: 14.05 h Cordoba-Seville.

CHART IV
SORTIES MADE BY THE FIRST JUNKERS JU 87V-4 *STUKA* (23-1) OUT OF THE AERODROMES OF TABLADA (SEVILLE) AND CORDOBA (CONTINUED)

JANUARY 1937

DATE	BULLETIN	PLACE	MOVEMENT AND SORTIES
JAN 02, 1937	Information bulletin No.16	Seville	10:10 h. 23-1 left on a special mission, bound for Cordoba, and returned at 14:40 h
			Cordoba Aerodrome Junkers 23-1 dive-bomber. Arrival: 14:40 h Seville-Cordoba. Junkers 23-1 dive-bomber. Departure: 10:50 h Arrival: 11:08 h Duration: 18 m
JAN 04, 1937	Information bulletin No.18	Seville	11:10 h. 23-1 arrived on a special mission from Cordoba.
			Cordoba Aerodrome. Junkers 23-1 dive-bomber. Departure: 09:50 h Cordoba-Seville.
JAN 05, 1937	Information bulletin No.19	Seville	10:20 h. 23-1 left for Cordoba, returning at 12:00 h
JAN 06, 1937	Information bulletin No.20	Seville	11:47 h. 23-1 left on a special mission and returned at 12:25 h
JAN 09, 1937	Information bulletin No.23	Seville	11:07 h.- Sale 23-1 left for Avila and returned at 16:20 h.
	Operations log, General HQ of the north. Air Force.	Avila	Reconnaissance aircraft 23-1 arrived from Seville at 11:55 h, leaving for the same place at 14:45 h

CHAPTER 3

The Junkers Ju 87A *Stuka*

The *Stuka Kette "Jolanthe"*

The production Junkers Ju 87As arrived in Spain in January 1938. They were incorporated in what was known as the *Stuka Kette "Jolanthe"*, so called because of the pig emblem of that name painted on the wheel fairings.

O n January 15, 1938 the first three production Junkers Ju 87A arrived in Spain and were assembled at the Leon Air Force Depot. These three aircraft came from *11. Staffel/LG 1*; in other words, from the 11th Squadron of Instruction Wing No.1, based at Barth. This *Luftwaffe* operational training unit had been equipped with the first production aircraft midway through 1937. *Oberstleutnant* Günther Schwartzkopff, the first firm believer and defender of the dive-bomber, had recommended that these aircraft be sent to Spain to be tested in actual combat missions, and the *Luftwaffe* Staff gave their blessing.

He was born in Forbach, near Posen, on August 5, 1898 and he may be said to have been one of the first to put his faith in the concept of the "dive-bomber." He has entered the annals of aviation history as the father of the "*Stukas*."

He took part in the First World War at only sixteen years of age and was wounded at the Battle of Verdun. After recovering from his wounds he transferred to the air force and after a period of training took part in a number of missions over the western and eastern fronts.

After the war he continued in the *Reichswehr* and in 1933 he joined the still clandestine *Luftwaffe*. He was promoted to the rank of *Hauptmann* and was transferred to the *Reichsluftfahrtministerium* (Air Ministry). In 1936 he was again promoted, to *Major*, and was sent to direct a flying school at Celle. Two years later, in January 1938, he was promoted yet again, this time to *Oberstleutnant*, and given the command of St.G 165, a group which would change its name in 1939 to officially become St.G 77.

He was responsible for testing the Ju 87s in combat as a tactical weapon and arrived in Spain in February 1938 to be present at their operational debut in the Civil War. He was attached to the Headquarters of J/88 with *Ausweis* No.366. He had no doubt that the *Stuka* units would be extraordinarily effective as an offensive weapon in the forthcoming war, as was demonstrated in the *Blitzkrieg*.

After serving with the St.G 77 group in the Polish campaign, he was transferred to the western front, flying in the operations carried out over France, Belgium and Holland. He was promoted to *Oberst* in April 1940.

On May 14 of that same year, during a mission in the Sedan area, his Junkers Ju 87 was shot down by anti-aircraft fire and he was killed instantly. He was posthumously promoted to *Generalmajor* and awarded the Knight's Cross of the Iron Cross.

Once the assembly of the trio of Junkers Ju 87As had been completed in Leon, on February 7 the aircraft were sent to the airfield at Calamocha (Teruel), initially under the name *Stuka Kette* or "Dive-Bomber Flight." This flight was led by *Leutnant* Hermann Haas. The unit was made up of the following aircraft and crews:

AIRCRAFT	REG. NO.	PILOT	RADIO
Ju 87A	29-4	*Lt.* Hermann Haas	*Fw.* Emil Kramer
Ju 87A	29-3	*Lt.* Gerhard Weyert	*Uffz.* Ernst Göller
Ju 87A	29-2	*Uffz.* Ernst Bartels	*Uffz.* Alfred Fleisch

We can see that these aircraft received type-number 29, but we know that the first Ju 87 to arrive in Spain a year earlier, the prototype V-4, had been type-numbered 23 and coded 23-1. What had happened to bring about this change of numbering? The explanation is simple. When the single example of this aircraft type was sent back to Germany, type-number 23 fell vacant, and in the summer of 1937 it was reassigned to the Italian twin-engined Fiat BR.20s. So, the Germans started the individual numbering of type-number 29 at 2, since there had already been an aircraft of that model coded 1, albeit with a different type-number. So the mystery is solved, once and for all.

Crewmembers of the *Stuka Kette*. From left to right we see *Uffz.* Fleisch (radio), *Uffz.* Bartels (pilot), *Fw.* Kramer (radio), *Maj.* Graf Flugger, of the Legion Condor Staff, *Ltn.* Weyert (pilot) and *Ltn.* Haas (pilot), the unit leader. Missing is *Uffz.* Göller (radio).

Painted on the fairings of the under-carriage of each aircraft in the *Kette* there was a common emblem, the *"Jolanthe,"* a chubby pig that was popular in Germany at that time.

Along with the flying crews, twenty technical staff had arrived from Germany to maintain the aircraft, including mechanics, armorers and ancillary staff. During the days following their arrival, the three dive-bombers attacked key targets in the Alfambra valley and on the Teruel front. Another hitherto unknown fact is that *Oberstleutnant* Schwartzkopff himself visited Spain at that time in order to see for himself how the *Stukas* performed in real combat conditions. In fact the first sorties by the *Stuka Kette* were flown between February 17 and 22, 1938. On the first day two sorties were made, their targets being enemy concentrations at Aldehuela and at the Teruel cemetery. On the following days, double or triple sorties were flown, depending on the day, over Valdecebro and Castralbo, Puebla de Valverde, Cobla, Aldehuela (again), the road to the south of Teruel, and against retreating columns of enemy tanks and trucks.

Above: The Junkers Ju 87 29-3 was crewed by Weyert and Göller.

Below: The Junkers Ju 87 29-4 was the mount of the leader of the *"Jolanthe" Stuka Kette*, *Leutnant* Hermann Haas. The unit was incorporated as the 5th Squadron of Fighter Group J./88.

	CHART V	
	OPERATIONS LOGS OF THE JUNKERS JU 87S A *STUKAS*	
	THE BATTLE OF TERUEL – ALFAMBRA	
	FEBRUARY 1938	
DATE	**UNIT**	**SORTIES**
FEB 17, 1938	J/88 Ju 87s	One sortie against enemy reserves at Aldehuela. Quantity of bombs: 0.5 tons. Second sortie, against enemy positions at cemetery. Quantity of bombs: 0.75 tons.
FEB 18, 1938	J/88	With Ju 87s, two sorties against retreating enemy at Valdecebro and Castralbo. 2.5 tons. Bombs on target.
FEB 19, 1938	J/88	With Ju 87s (3), sortie against retreating enemy positions at cemetery. Bombs on target.
FEB 20, 1938	J/88	Three Ju 87s, one sortie each, with goods results, against enemy concentrations to the east of Villaespesa. 1.5 tons.
FEB 21, 1938	J/88 with Ju 87s (3)	First sortie, road and railway bridges to the northwest of Puebla de Valverde. 0.7 tons, near target. Second sortie, against enemy movements at Cobla. 0.7 tons on target. Explosions were observed. Enemy defense by fighters.
FEB 22, 1938	J/88 with Ju 87s	First sortie (3), against Aldehuela. Two bombs on target. Second sortie (2), against tanks on the road to the south of Teruel. One hit on the road. Third sortie (2), against moving columns, which were tanks and trucks. Two hits on the road. Three trucks were seen to explode. In total, 1.7 tons.

The 5.J/88

The Calamocha airfield was home to the Legion Condor's Fighter Group J/88, then equipped with two squadrons of Messerschmitt Bf 109 monoplanes (1. and 2.J/88) and a further two squadrons (3. and 4.J/88) of Heinkel He 51 biplanes, relegated by then to a ground support role. For administration purposes, the *Stuka Kette* was incorporated into J/88 and became squadron 5.J/88. In March 1938 operations began over the Aragon front and the Ju 87 unit continued to fly sorties. One day, before the Aragon operations had begun (the exact date is not known), it seems that one of the Ju 87s, number 29-3 to be precise, suffered a mishap and was forced to land in a field in the vicinity of Belchite. On the back of a photo of the above mentioned aircraft, there is a note to that effect and the aeronautical historian Jesús Salas Larrazábal, on page 317 of his book *"La Guerra de España desde el Aire"* ("The Spanish War from the Air"), mentions the loss of a Ju 87 in the Bujaraloz sector. It was then when a fourth Ju 87A arrived from Germany, which was given the code number 29-5.

Above: The Ju 87A 29-3 had to make a forced landing in a field close to Belchite.

Below: The *Stuka* 29-4 undergoes some maintenance work.

With regard to the controversial aircraft coded 29-6, everything would seem to point to the fact that it did not exist. The accounts of the Legion Condor are clear in this respect. Only twelve Junkers Ju 87s in total arrived in Spain, including the V-4 prototype. By our reckoning, in addition to the V-4, there were four Ju 87A and seven Ju 87B aircraft in Spain, as we will see later in this book. Another argument in support of our claim is that there is no documentary or photographic evidence of the "phantom" 29-6, while of all the other aircraft there are plenty of photographs to prove their existence.

Returning now to the offensive of the Aragon front, on March 6 two *Stukas* dive-bombed the bridge over the Ebro at Sástago without success, since the bombs fell wide of the target. These air raids were carried out with an escort of Messerschmitt Bf 109 fighters from J/88, but only at Caspe were any enemy fighters seen: three Polikarpov I-16 "Mosca" monoplanes, which made a vain attempt to attack the bombers.

The following day, at 13:00h, all the bombers of K/88 (He 111) and A/88 (Do 17), accompanied by a covering escort of German fighters, began to bomb the station at Puebla de Híjar. Meanwhile the three Ju 87s bombed the bridge at Sástago again, without destroying the target.

Above: A fourth Junkers Ju 87A was sent to Spain to cover lost or unserviceable aircraft and other eventualities. It was coded as 29-5.

Center: *Unteroffizier* Bartels was the pilot of Ju 87 *Stuka* number 29-2. He is photographed with his mascot, a teddy bear.

Below: Photo of the aforementioned aircraft of the 5.J/88, crewed by Bartels and Fleisch.

The 5.J/88 operated over the Aragon front in March 1938.

On March 8, since the "*Jolanthe Kette*" had been unsuccessful, two squadrons of Heinkel He 111s belonging to K/88 took off, bound for the same target. The twin-engined bombers attacked the bridge over the Ebro at Sástago at a height of less than fifty meters, but despite hitting both ends of the span, they failed to totally destroy the bridge. Two Ju 87s of 5.J/88 squadron succeeded in dropping two 500kg bombs on the railway embankment to the east of Puebla de Híjar, thereby cutting the Saragossa-Alcañiz railway route. On March 9, the *Kette* of Ju 87s, with fighter escort, made another three sorties against enemy positions and concentrations at Azuara and Casilta, 6km to the west of Belchite, dropping 3.15 tons of bombs and scoring some good hits.

On the tenth of the month, four sorties were flown against enemy concentrations at Belchite and against the crossroads to the east of the town, during which a total of 4.5 tons of bombs were dropped. The following day the flight known as "*Jolanthe Kette*," with its Ju 87s, made a sortie against the crossroads at Azaila, dropping their bombs on target.

On March 12, at noon, 5.J/88 squadron, with its three Junkers Ju 87, bombed the railway station at Azaila and a number of enemy concentrations at Sástago, scoring hits on the station building and the railway lines out of Azaila, and the town of

Sástago. They also hit the rearguard of the government troops, leaving them cut off. Then on the 15th the three *Stukas* flew two missions each against the road bridge to the southeast of Caspe and while the bombs fell very near the target, they failed to accomplish their mission of destroying the bridge, although traffic was interrupted for a short time.

These sorties were made with an escort of two squadrons of Bf 109s, which also escorted A/88 squadron. The next day, at around 15:00h, an attempt was made to break the defensive line at Maella with a squadron of Heinkel He 111s, albeit without success. Previously the *Stukas*, escorted by Bf 109 fighters, had bombed a number of enemy batteries at Caspe and a munitions column on the road from Maella. In the course of these raids, around thirty enemy Polikarpov I-15 "Chato" fighters appeared but did not attack, allowing the Germans to withdraw without incident.

5.J/88 squadron remained inactive until March 22 when the Ju 87s attacked reinforced cement bunkers to the north of Lierta. On the 25th the aircraft of the *Stuka Kette* scored a direct hit on an ammunition dump during their first sortie and on their second they bombed the crossroads to the northwest of Alcalá del Obispo. The raid was a complete success, although the traffic was not interrupted for long since the Republicans simply diverted it cross-country, around the bottleneck created by the bombing.

Above: In the photo we can see in detail the *"Jolanthe"* pig emblem painted on the wheel fairing.

Below: This Junkers Ju 87A bears the pilot's personal bowler and umbrella emblem on the undercarriage fairings.

On the following days the Ju 87 was operating over the Huesca and Lérida front, especially at Monzón and Fraga. On March 29, in two sorties, the fuel depots to the west of Lerida were attacked and set ablaze, as was the vehicle park to the northeast of the city. The second sortie attracted the attention of enemy fighters but no loss or damage was reported.

Early in April the *Stukas'* targets were centered on communication nodes at Lerida, Balaguer and Tremp. The rest of the month, until the 21st, 5.J/88 flew no more sorties.

Above: The *Stukas* delivered this magnificent precision hit on the crossroads at Alcalá del Obispo.

Below: The SC 250 bombs used by the Ju 87A *Stukas* were 1.64 m long in total.

Chart VI
The Aragon offensive

March 1938

Date	Unit	Sorties
Mar 06, 1938	J/88 with Ju 87s	Sortie against bridges over the Ebro at Sástago. 1 ton. Bombs near target.
Mar 07, 1938	J/88 with Ju 87s	Sortie against the bridge at Sástago. 0.7 tons near target.
Mar 08, 1938	J/88 with Ju 87s	Sortie against the railway line to the east of Puebla de Híjar. 0.7 tons, hitting the line.
Mar 09, 1938	J/88 with Ju 87s (3)	Four sorties against enemy positions and concentrations at Azuara and Casilta, 6 km to the west of Belchite. 3.15 tons. Bombs well placed.
Mar 10, 1938	J/88 with two squadrons Bf 109s	Escort for K/88, A/88, He 51s and Ju 87s.
Mar 10, 1938	J/88 with three Ju 87s	Four sorties against enemy concentrations at Belchite and crossroads to the east. 4.5 tons. Bombs well placed.
Mar 11, 1938	J/88 with Ju 87s (3)	Sortie against crossroads at Azaila. 2.5 tons. Bombs on target.

CHART VI		
THE ARAGON OFFENSIVE (CONTINUED)		
MARCH 1938		
DATE	**UNIT**	**SORTIES**
MAR 12, 1938	J/88 with two squadrons Bf 109s	Escort for K/88, A/88, He 51s and Ju 87s.
MAR 12, 1938	Three Ju 87s	Each made one sortie against Azaila station and enemy concentrations at Sástago. 2 tons. Hits on station building and tracks at Azail and on the town of Sástago.
MAR 15, 1938	J/88 with two squadrons Bf 109s	Escort for A/88 and Ju 87s.
MAR 15, 1938	Three Ju 87s	Two sorties against road bridge to the southeast of Caspe. Very close to target.
MAR 16, 1938	J/88 with two squadrons Bf 109s	Escort for K/88 and Ju 87s.
MAR 16, 1938	Three Ju 87s	Sortie against enemy field battery to the north of Caspe. Two hits on the battery.
MAR 16, 1938	Two Ju 87s	Sortie against column of trucks to the southeast of Caspe. 2x500 kg. In total, 2.5 tons.

CHART VI
THE ARAGON OFFENSIVE (CONTINUED)

MARCH 1938

DATE	UNIT	SORTIES
MAR 22, 1938	J/88 with two squadrons Bf 109s	Escort for K/88, A/88, He 51s and Ju 87s.
MAR 22, 1938	With three Ju 87s	Sortie against reinforced cement positions to the north of Lierta. 1 ton near target.
MAR 24, 1938	J/88 with two squadrons Bf 109s	Escort for bombers.
MAR 24, 1938	With Ju 87s (3)	First sortie against crossroads at Apiés and second sortie against crossroads to the northwest of Igriés. 2.5 tons on target.
MAR 25, 1938	J/88. With three Ju 87s	One sortie against SESA (explosion of an ammunition dump) and against crossroads to the northwest of Alcalá del Obispo. Bombs well placed. According to our own intelligence, during the night there were still explosions at SESA.
MAR 26, 1938	J/88. With three Ju 87s	Sortie against the station at Monzón. 1.25 tons. Bombs well placed.
MAR 27, 1938	J/88. With two squadrons Bf 109s	Six escort sorties for K/88, A/88 and Ju 87s.

	CHART VI	
	THE ARAGON OFFENSIVE (CONTINUED)	
	MARCH 1938	
DATE	UNIT	SORTIES
MAR 27, 1938	Ju 87 (3)	Two sorties against enemy concentrations on the road leaving Fraga to the west. 2.5 tons on target.
MAR 28, 1938	J./88.- Con dos Ju 87	Sorties against railway line Monzón-Lérida. I ton near target.
MAR 29, 1938	J./88	Escort for K/88, A/88 and Ju 87s.
MAR 29, 1938	Ju 87 (2)	Two sorties against CAMPSA [fuel depot] and vehicle depot to the northeast of Lerida. In the first sortie, good placement of bombs. In the second sortie there was enemy fighter defense. According to our observation, the CAMPSA depot continued burning through the night.
MAR 30, 1938	J./88.- Con Bf 109	Escort for bombers.
MAR 30, 1938	Con Ju 87 (3)	First sortie, against concentrations of trucks near Alcarraz. Second sortie, to cut the road to La Einsa-Arro. I ton.
APR 02, 1938	J./88.- Con Bf 109	Escort for K/88 and Ju 87s.
APR 02, 1938	Con Ju 87	Sorties against two buildings (Staff HQ) to the east of Lerida. I ton near target.

CHART VI
THE ARAGON OFFENSIVE (CONTINUED)

APRIL 1938

DATE	UNIT	SORTIES
APR 04, 1938	J/88 Ju 87s	No sortie.
APR 05, 1938	J/88. With two squadrons Bf 109s	Two escort sorties for K/88, A/88 and Ju 87s.
APR 05, 1938	With two Ju 87s	Sortie against crossroads to the southeast of Balaguer. 1 ton near target.
APR 06, 1938	J/88. With two squadrons	Escort for K/88, A/88 and Ju 87s.
APR 06, 1938	With three Ju 87s	One sortie to blow up the road leading south of Tremp. 1.5 tons. Once 500 kg hit the road leaving the town.
APR 07, 1938	J/88 Ju 87s	No sortie.
APR 10, 1938	J/88 Bf 109s and Ju 87s	No sortie.
APR 12, 1938	J/88 Bf 109s and Ju 87s	No sortie.
APR 12, 1938	J/88 Ju 87s	No sortie.

Destination La Cenia (Tarragona)

With the Republican territory split into two after the seaborne arrival of Nationalist troops at Vinaroz (Castellón), on April 21 Group J/88 of the Legion Condor transferred to the recently occupied airfield at La Cenia in the southernmost part of the province of Tarragona. This airfield had been the headquarters of Republican Air Force Group 24, made up of twin-engined Tupolev SB "Katiuska" aircraft, and its capture allowed German planes to operate on either the Levante or Catalonian fronts, giving it a fundamental strategic importance. 5.J/88 squadron moved there too, and their personnel was billeted in a requisitioned villa in a nearby village. The operational debut of the *Stuka* from their new base took place on April 25 with an attack on enemy concentrations at Cuevas de Vinromá. The following day

Above: The formerly Republican held aerodrome of La Cenia (Tarragona) was the permanent base of 5.J/88 from April 1938 until it was disbanded.

the same target was attacked again in two sorties in which 2.25 tons of bombs were dropped. The next mission would not be flown until May 4 when Torreblanca was attacked and three hits were scored. On the 15th the Ju 87s returned to attack Cuevas, but had to turn back due to bad weather. On May 18 and 19 the targets were Albocácer and Ares del

The towns of Benasal and Vilar de Canes, in the Sierra del Maestrazgo mountains, were both *Stuka* targets. They were attacked with SC 500J bombs; at 1.97 m long these bombs were taller than a man.

Previous page, bottom: Yesterday and today. The aircrews of the *Stuka Kette "Jolanthe"* were billeted in this villa in the town of La Cenia.

Maestre, which they attacked again on the 24th and the 28th. On the 26th a sortie was flown against Vilar de Canes, a hard to reach village in the Sierra del Maestrazgo mountains. Another of the prime targets for the 28th was Benasal, where a major concentration of enemy vehicles was attacked using 500kg bombs. Early in June 1938 the targets were Benlloch, Villar de Canes, Benasal, Albocácer and Azdaneta. On the 9th the Ju 87As bombed anti-aircraft batteries at Villafamés, scoring two hits. On consecutive days the *Stuka Kette* operated over Borriol, Villafamés, Villareal, Alcora and Artana, where on the 28th and 29th, the prime target were enemy artillery batteries. On the following day the Ju 87s had to turn back due to bad weather.

Moving forward to July, the Nationalists attempted to take Valencia, and the *Stukas* of 5.J/88 squadron attacked a communications node at Nules and a train to the northwest of Amposta on the 4th. On the 8th, an ammunition dump at Vall de Uxó was bombed, with the bombs falling very close to the target. On July 14, the Ju 87s attacked enemy positions in the Sierra de Espadán mountains, which were again the target on the 15th and 18th of the month. There were no further sorties over the Levante front until the 24th, when four sorties were flown against the crossroads near Rasquera, where the bombs fell close to the target.

Above: Inspection of a Junkers Ju 87 engine.

Below: A crewmember of a *Stuka* prepares to climb into the cockpit.

The "Devil's Head" (*Teufelskopf*) emblem which decorated the Hs 123 of the *Stuka Kette 88*.

Above: The first two Henschel Hs 123 flew in Spain with this gray livery of the *Luftwaffe* and with code numbers 501 and 502.

Henschel Hs 123 coded 24-2 of the *Stuka Kette 88*. This aircraft was decorated with the pilot's own skull and crossbones (*Totenkopf*) emblem.

Detail of the skull and crossbones emblem.

65

Above: The prototype V-4 of the Junkers Ju 87 *Stuka* at the Rechlin Test Center bore the civil air registration number D-UBIP.

Center: After being sent to Spain in December 1936, the Ju 87V-4 was assigned the type-number 23, and with code number 23-1 operated mainly over the Cordoba front in late December 1936 and early January 1937.

Center right: Flag of the Legion Condor.

Below: The type-number of the first three production Junkers Ju 87A was changed to 29. This aircraft in particular was the first one to be received.

The Ju 87A coded 29-3 had a bowler hat and umbrella emblem painted on its undercarriage fairings.

Detail of the emblem.

The Junkers Ju 87 29-4 was the aircraft piloted by *Ltn.* Hermann Haas, leader of *Stuka Kette* 5/J.88. It was decorated with the official emblem of the unit, the Jolanthe pig.

The Ju 87 coded 29-5 was the last of the series: a aircraft sent to Spain to cover lost or unserviceable aircraft.

The pink Jolanthe pig on an oval background was the official emblem of the Junkers Ju 87 *Stuka*.

Uffz. Ernst Bartels piloted the Junkers Ju 87 coded 29-2. Note the teddy bear he carried as a mascot in the aircraft's cockpit.

Bartels' Ju 87 *Stuka* starts its dive to
bomb a target on the Ebro front.

Under the burning summer sun at La Cenia, a German mechanic inspects a Ju 87.

A German *Leutnant*, crewmember of a
Junkers Ju 87, in service uniform.

Above: The Junkers Ju 87B 29-8 of *Stuka.* K./88 was the only one of its type to be shot down by an enemy fighter, although it was not destroyed.

Detail of the Jolanthe pig with red trim.

Center: Junkers Ju 87B coded 29-11 of *Stuka* K./88 during the Catalonian campaign.

Right: One of the Junkers Ju 87Bs in Spain, code unknown, had the name "Peterle" painted on the engine cover. The name is a diminutive form of Peter; comparable to "Pete" in English.

Below: The Junkers Ju 87B coded 29-13 was the last to be sent to Spain, to cover lost or unserviceable aircraft. In total twelve Ju 87s arrived in Spain: the prototype V-4, four A-series, and seven B-series.

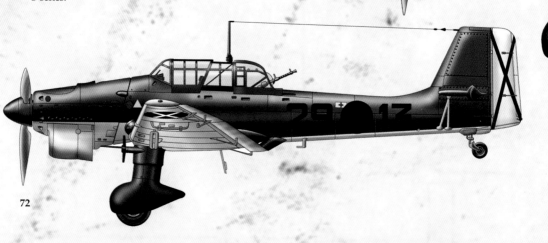

CHART VII
OPERATIONS ON THE LEVANTE FRONT

APRIL 1938

DATE	UNIT	SORTIES
APR 21, 1938	J/88	Move to the coast. (La Cenia)
APR 25, 1938	J/88 Ju 87s (3)	Sortie against enemy concentrations at Cuevas. 1.25 tons. All bombs on target.
APR 26, 1938	J/88 With Bf 109s	Two escort sorties for Ju 87s.
APR 26, 1938	Ju 87s (3)	Two sorties against enemy concentrations at Cuevas. 2.25 tons. Bombs well placed.
MAY 04, 1938	J/88 Ju 87s	One sortie against Torreblanca and three hits.
MAY 15, 1938	J/88 With Bf 109s	One free-range fighter sortie in the Vinaroz sector and escort for Ju 87s.
MAY 15, 1938	With three Ju 87s	One sortie against Cuevas. The sortie was interrupted due to bad weather.
MAY 18, 1938	J/88 With Bf 109s	Eleven escort sorties for K/88, A/88 and Ju 87s.

The Junkers Ju 87A carried camouflage markings in three colors: green, gray and tan.

CHART VII
OPERATIONS ON THE LEVANTE FRONT (CONTINUED)

MAY 1938

DATE	UNIT	SORTIES
MAY 18, 1938	Ju 87s (3)	Three sorties against enemy concentrations at Albocácer. One sortie against enemy positions to the north of Ares del Maestre. Six tons. Good bomb placement (one bomb failed to explode).
MAY 19, 1938	J/88 With 3 Ju 87s	One sortie against Albocácer. 1.5 tons. Three hits.
MAY 24, 1938	J/88. With Bf 109s	Escort for A/88, He 51s and Ju 87s.
MAY 24, 1938	Ju 87s	Two sorties against Ares del Maestre. Three tons. Five hits.

Crewmembers and
ground staff are
photographed around a
Junkers Ju 87 of 5.J/88.

CHART VII

OPERATIONS ON THE LEVANTE FRONT (CONTINUED)

	MAY 1938	
DATE	**UNIT**	**SORTIES**
MAY 25, 1938	J/88 With Bf 109s	Escort for bomber sections and Ju 87s.
MAY 25, 1938	Ju 87s	Sortie against Benasal. 1.5 tons. Bombs on target.
MAY 26, 1938	J/88 With Bf 109s	Escort for A/88 bombers and Ju 87s.
MAY 26, 1938	With Ju 87s	Sortie against Villar de Canes. 1.5 tons. Good bomb placement.
MAY 28, 1938	J/88 With Bf 109s	Four sorties with Ju 87s.
MAY 28, 1938	Ju 87s	One sortie against Arés del Maestre (sic), three times, 500 kg. Two hits. Against Benasal, three times 500 kg. Two hits. Against Albocácer, twice 500 kg. One hit. Against Benasal, three times 500 kg. Three hits.
MAY 29, 1938	J/88 With Bf 109s	Escort for bomber sections.
MAY 29, 1938	Ju 87s (3)	One sortie each against Albocácer and enemy positions on the Arés heights. Three tons. Good bomb placement.
MAY 31, 1938	J/88 With Bf 109s	Escort for bomber sections.
MAY 31, 1938	With three Ju 87s	Sorties against Villar de Canes and Saratella. Three tons and three hits.

Above: Ju 87 29-3, with its engine cowling removed, undergoes some repairs.

Below: A crew of armorers belonging to 5.J/88 prepare to fit a 250 kilo bomb to the ETC 500/IX bomb rack used by the *Stukas*.

Ju 87 29-5 was the last of the A-series to operate in Spain.
There was no aircraft coded 29-6.

An *Unteroffizier* of the
Legion Condor poses in
front of Junkers Ju 87,
29-3.

Chart VII
Operations on the Levante front (Continued)

June 1938

Date	Unit	Sorties
Jun 01, 1938	J/88 With Bf 109s	Escort for bomber sections.
Jun 01, 1938	With three Ju 87s	Sorties against Benlloch. Three sorties, twice with three and once with one, against enemy positions on the heights 7 km to the south of Villar de Canes. In total, 5.5 tons. Seven hits. Two bombs near target. One failed to explode.
Jun 02, 1938	J/88 With Bf 109s	Escort for bomber sections.
Jun 02, 1938	With three Ju 87s	Two sorties against enemy positions to the southeast of Benasal. One sortie against enemy positions to the southeast of Albocácer. 4.5 tons. Bombs well placed.
Jun 03, 1938	J/88 With Bf 109s	Escort for bomber sections and A/88.
Jun 03, 1938	Ju 87s	Four sorties against enemy positions on the heights to the north of Villar de Canes and to the south of Torre de Embesora. 6 tons. Bombs well placed.
Jun 07, 1938	J/88 With Bf 109s	Escort for bomber sections and A/88.
Jun 07, 1938	Ju 87s	Sortie against enemy positions to the southeast of Azdaneta. Two sorties against the Albocácer-La Barona road. 6 tons. Bombs well placed. One bomb failed to explode.

CHART VII
LAS OPERACIONES EN EL FRENTE DE LEVANTE (CONTINUED)

JUNE 1938

DATE	UNIT	SORTIES
JUN 08, 1938	J/88 With Bf 109s	Escort and protection for all the sorties of K/88, A/88 and Ju 87s.
JUN 08, 1938	Ju 87s	One sortie against road near Barona. 1.5 tons. Bombs well placed.
JUN 09, 1938	J/88 With Bf 109s	Fighter protection for bomber sections.
JUN 09, 1938	Ju 87s	Two sorties, with three Ju 87s, against anti-aircraft battery emplacements near Villafamés. 3 tons. Two hits. One sortie, with three Ju 87s, against enemy positions to the west of Costur. 1.5 tons. Three hits.
JUN 10, 1938	J/88	Escort for A/88 and Ju 87s, with Bf 109s.
JUN 10, 1938	Ju 87s (3)	Sorties against enemy positions to the northeast of Villafamés. 1.5 tons. Bombs well placed.
JUN 11, 1938	J/88 With Bf 109s	Escort for bomber sections and Ju 87s.
JUN 11, 1938	With three Ju 87s	Sortie against intersection near Borriol. 1.5 tons. Three hits.

CHART VII
OPERATIONS ON THE LEVANTE FRONT (CONTINUED)

JUNE 1938

DATE	UNIT	SORTIES
JUN 12, 1938	J/88 With Bf 109s	Escort for bomber sections and A/88.
JUN 12, 1938	Ju 87s	Sortie against stretch of road near Villarreal. 1 ton. One hit.
JUN 13, 1938	J/88 With Bf 109s	Protection for bomber sections, A/88 and Ju 87s.
JUN 13, 1938	With three Ju 87s	Two sorties against stretches of road and station at Nules and Villarreal. 4 tons. Hits on and near road. Explosions observed.
JUN 14, 1938	J/88 With Bf 109s	Escort for bomber sections and A/88.
JUN 14, 1938	With Ju 87s	Sortie against enemy positions 7 km to the south of Alcora. 1.5 tons. Bombs on target.
JUN 28, 1938	J/88 With Bf 109s	Escort for A/88 and Ju 87s.
JUN 28, 1938	With three Ju 87s	Sortie against battery to the west of Artena. 1.5 tons. Three bombs on the suspected site of the battery.

CHART VII
OPERATIONS ON THE LEVANTE FRONT (CONTINUED)

JUNE 1938

DATE	UNIT	SORTIES
JUN 29, 1938	J/88. With Bf 109s	Escort for A/88 and Ju 87s.
JUN 29, 1938	Ju 87s	First sortie against positions to the west of Onda. 1 ton. Effects could not be observed. Second sortie against artillery positions near Artena. Half a ton. The battery emplacement could not be reconnoitered. Smoke observed at the point where the battery was suspected to be.
JUN 30, 1938	J/88	With Bf 109s, escort for A/88 and Ju 87s.
JUN 30, 1938	Ju 87s	The sortie was interrupted due to bad weather.

JULY 1938

DATE	UNIT	SORTIES
JUL 01, 1938	J/88 With Bf 109s	Escort for A/88 and Ju 87s.
JUL 01, 1938	With Ju 87s	Sortie against the intersection at Nules. 1 ton. Smoke observed.
JUL 04, 1938	J/88 With Bf 109s	Protection for bomber sections, A/88 and Ju 87s.
JUL 04, 1938	With two Ju 87s	Two sorties against train to the northwest of Amposta. 2 tons. Three bombs beside the target. One bomb failed to explode next to the target.

CHART VII
OPERATIONS ON THE LEVANTE FRONT (CONTINUED)

JULY 1938

DATE	UNIT	SORTIES
JUL 08, 1938	J/88 Bf 109s	*Begleigtung bombevervande und Aufklaer.* Protection for bomber sections and reconnaissance.
JUL 08, 1938	Ju 87s	*87 ein maliger einsatz auf munitionslager bei Vall Uxó. ½ To. Bomben in der nahe des ziel.* ... One sortie against an ammunition dump at Vall de Uxó. 0.5 tons. Bombs beside the target.
JUL 10, 1938	J/88 With 3 Ju 87s	Sorties against observation posts on hills 2 km to the southwest of Torralba. 1.5 tons. Column of smoke on the heights.
JUL 14, 1938	J/88 Bf 109s	*Begleigtung K, Ju 87s und einmal Aufklaer.* Escort for Group K and Ju 87s.
JUL 14, 1938	Ju 87s (3)	*Angriff auf Sierra Espadán. 1 ½ To. Gute Bombenlage.* Attack on Sierra de Espadán. 1.5 tons. Good bomb placement.
JUL 15, 1938	J/88 Bf 109s	*Begleigtung bombevervande und Ju 87s.* Escort for bomber section and Ju 87s.
JUL 15, 1938	Ju 87s	Attack on Sierra de Espadán. 1.5 tons. Bombs on target.

CHART VII
OPERATIONS ON THE LEVANTE FRONT (CONTINUED)

JULY 1938

DATE	UNIT	SORTIES
JUL 18, 1938	J/88 Bf 109s	*Begleigtung bombevervande und Ju 87s.* Escort for bomber section and Ju 87s.
JUL 18, 1938	Ju 87s	*Zweimaliger angriff (Je3) auf feindstellugen Sierra Espadán. 3 To.* Attacked enemy positions at Sierra de Espadán three times. 3 tons.
JUL 20, 1938	J/88 Ju 87s	No sorties.
JUL 22, 1938	J/88 Ju 87s	No sorties.
JUL 24, 1938	J/88 With Bf 109s	Escort for bomber sections and Ju 87s.
JUL 24, 1938	Ju 87s (4)	Sortie against the intersection near Rasquera. Bombs near target.

Bomb trolley for SC 250 bombs.

The Hard-fought Battle of the Ebro

The Nationalist offensive against Valencia was rudely interrupted by the surprise river crossing over the Ebro by the Republican Popular Army on July 25, 1938. The Junkers Ju 87s of 5.J/88 squadron then changed their operational front and on July 26 began operations with four sorties of three Ju 87s, escorted by Bf 109s, against the crossroads at Venta de Camposines and the bridge near Ginestar. In these actions they dropped six tons of bombs to good effect. On the 27th they flew another four sorties, attacking Venta de Camposines once again and bombing a concentration of tanks at Corbera and some pontoons being used by troops to cross the river in the area of Vinebre, scoring a number of direct hits. On the following days the *Stukas* continued to fly sorties against concentrations of enemy troops at Pinell, Ginestar, Corbera and an air observation post near Tortosa. The bridges at

Above: Pair of Junkers Ju 87 at the La Cenia aerodrome.

Below: The entire *Stuka Kette "Jolanthe"* takes off, simultaneously, from the La Cenia aerodrome.

Asc& and Vinebre were also attacked, the latter target being hit, as was the railway tunnel to the east of Mora la Nueva. Another sortie against this latter masonry structure was made on August 1 and its southernmost portal received a hit.

During these early days of August sortie after sortie was made against bridges and troop concentrations at the aforementioned places. It would be monotonous and repetitive to recount one by one all the sorties flown by the Ju 87As of 5.J/88 squadron during the following months of August and September 1938 in the Ebro sector. Suffice to say, these German dive-bombers flew practically every day, as a rule making two or three sorties a day. They scored

Above: The ground echelon prepares a Ju 87 for a mission.

Below: La Cenia aerodrome covered a considerable area.

Above: A pair of Ju 87s in flight over the Ebro sector.

Below: Another photo, in flight, of a Ju 87A over the arid Aragonese desert.

notable successes, although the method was not infallible and the bombs dropped from the *Stukas* did not always go off, as we can see in the list of sorties that we reproduce in the corresponding text box. These sorties were carried out with an escort of Messerschmitt Bf 109s and although they sometimes attacked in the presence of enemy fighters and under anti-aircraft fire, no Ju 87 suffered any damage from either.

	CHART VIII	
	BATTLE OF THE EBRO	
	JULY 1938	
DATE	**UNIT**	**SORTIES**
Jul 26, 1938	J/88. With Bf 109s	On escort duties for bomber sections and the Ju 87s.
Jul 26, 1938	With three Ju 87s	Four sorties against the intersection at Venta de Camposines and bridge near Ginestar. 6 tons. Bombs very well placed on the crossroads and roads.
Jul 27, 1938	J/88. With Bf 109s	Escort for K/88 and Ju 87s in four sorties.
Jul 27, 1938	Ju 87s	First sortie: With three aircraft against the intersection near Venta de Camposines. Apparently one bomb on target. Second sortie: With three Ju 87s, against concentration of tanks at Corbera. Hit on the road out of the village. Third sortie: With three Ju 87s, against the intersection near Venta de Camposines. Traffic on Mora de Ebro road halted due to hits. Fourth. With three Ju 87s against attempt by enemy to cross the Ebro at Vinebre. Hit on occupied pontoons. Fire observed. In total, 6 tons.

CHART VIII
BATTLE OF THE EBRO (CONTINUED)

JULY 1938

DATE	UNIT	SORTIES
JUL 28, 1938	J/88. With Bf 109s	Escort for bomber sections, Ju 87s and the reconnaissance flight, in four sorties.
JUL 28, 1938	With three Ju 87s	Sortie against concentrations at Pinell. 1.5 tons. Bombs well placed.
JUL 29, 1938	J/88. With Bf 109s	Escort for bomber sections and Ju 87s, in six sorties.
JUL 29, 1938	Ju 87s (3)	Sorties against concentrations at Pinell and bridge near Ginestar. 3 tons. One bomb on Pinell. Hits on the east and west banks of the Ebro, beside the bridge.
JUL 30, 1938	J/88. With Bf 109s	Escort for bomber sections and Ju 87s in five sorties.
JUL 30, 1938	Ju 87s	Two sorties against concentrations at Corbera, and against bridges near Ascó and Vinebre. 4 tons on Corbera. Hit on bridge at Vinebre.

Chart VIII
Battle of the Ebro (Continued)

July 1938

Date	Aircraft	Sorties
Jul 31, 1938	J/88. With Bf 109s	Escort of the A/88 bombers and Ju 87s, in four sorties.
Jul 31, 1938	With two Ju 87s	First sortie against an air observation post to the east of Tortosa. 1 ton. Bombs on either side of the target. Second sortie, with three Ju 87s, against tunnel exit 4 km to the east of Mora la Nueva. 1.5 tons. Bomb on top of tunnel, but failed to destroy it. Third sortie, with three Ju 87s, against concentrations at Corbera, to prevent a counterattack. 1.5 tons. Two bombs on target. One bomb on the southern slope of the hill.

August 1938

Date	Aircraft	Sorties
Aug 01, 1938	J/88. With Bf 109s	Escort for bomber sections and Ju 87s in two sorties.
Aug 01, 1938	Ju 87s	First sortie, with three Ju 87s, against a tunnel 5 km to the east of Mora la Nueva. 1.5 tons. Hit on road out of village to the south. Another two bombs on either side of the road out to the north. Second sortie, with three Ju 87s, against concentrations at Rasquera. 1.5 tons. Two bombs on target. One bomb to the east of the target.

CHART VIII
BATTLE OF THE EBRO (CONTINUED)

AUGUST 1938		
AUG 01, 1938	J/88. With Bf 109s	Escort for bomber sections and Ju 87s, in three sorties.
AUG 01, 1938	Ju 87s	First sortie, with three Ju 87s, against a 5 km tunnel east of Mora la Nueva. 1.5 tons. White off the south. Other two pumps on both sides of the North exit. Second sortie, with three Ju 87s, against Rasquera concentrations. 1.5 tons. Two pumps in white. A bomb in the east of the target.

Ground staff at La Cenia with trolleys carrying bombs for the *Stukas*.

CHART VIII

CHART VIII
BATTLE OF THE EBRO (CONTINUED)

AUGUST 1938

DATE	UNIT	SORTIES
AUG 02, 1938	J/88. With Bf 109s	Escort for bomber sections and Ju 87s, in three sorties.
AUG 02, 1938	Ju 87s	First sortie, with three Ju 87s, against concentrations at Corbera. 1.5 tons. Two bombs on target, one to the side. Second sortie, with three Ju 87s, against the little bridge to the southeast of Ginestar-Miravet. 1.5 tons. Hit on the little bridge.
AUG 03, 1938	J/88. With Bf 109s	Escort for bomber sections and Ju 87s, in three sorties.
AUG 03, 1938	Ju 87s	First sortie, with three Ju 87s, against the part of the bridge on land to the east of Benifallet. One bomb on the road and two off-target. Second sortie, with three Ju 87s, against concentrations at Ginestar. 1.5 tons. One bomb on target. Second and third to the south and northeast of the beach at Ginestar. Third sortie, with three Ju 87s, against a road at Rasquera. 1.5 tons. One bomb on the outskirts to the west, one on the western part of the town, and one off-target.
AUG 04, 1938	J/88 Ju 87s	No sorties.
AUG 05, 1938	J/88 Ju 87s	No sorties.

91

CHART VIII BATTLE OF THE EBRO (CONTINUED)		
AUGUST 1938		
DATE	UNIT	SORTIES
AUG 06, 1938	J/88. With Bf 109s	Escort for K/88 and Ju 87s and reconnaissance flight in three sorties.
AUG 06, 1938	Ju 87s	First sortie, with three Ju 87s, against cut bridge to the northeast of Ginestar. 1.5 tons. Second sortie, with three Ju 87s, the same as the first. Two bombs to the west of the bridge. One bomb failed to explode. Third sortie, same as the first. 1.5 tons. One bomb on the bridge, on the land part. Two bombs near bridge.
AUG 07, 1938	J/88. With Bf 109s	Escort for K/88, Ju 87s and A. in four sorties.
AUG 07, 1938	Ju 87s	First sortie, with three Ju 87s, against little bridge to the west of Ginestar. 1.5 tons. The little bridge was very twisted. According to intelligence, completely cut shortly after. Second sortie, the same as the first. 1.5 tons. One bomb on the west part and another on the east part of the bridge, on the land part. One bomb on Benifallet. Third sortie, with three Ju 87s, against the land part of the bridge to the south of Mora de Ebro. 1.5 tons. One bomb on the road, another two could not be seen due to heavy cloud cover.
AUG 08, 1938	J/88. With Bf 109s	Escort for bomber sections, Ju 87s and reconnaissance flight, in two sorties.
AUG 05, 1938	Ju 87s	With three aircraft, sortie against little bridge to the west of Benifallet. 1.5 tons. Bombs missed target.

Chart VIII
Battle of the Ebro (Continued)

August 1938

Date	Unit	Sorties
Aug 09, 1938	J/88. With Bf 109s	Escort for K/88 and Ju 87s and free range fighters. Four sorties.
Aug 09, 1938	Ju 87s	First sortie, with three Ju 87s, against little bridge to the west of Benifallet. 1.5 tons. Two bombs near target. One bomb on the road out of the town. Second sortie, with three Ju 87s, like the first. Bombs on the road into the town. Two bombs near target. Enemy anti-aircraft defense. Third sortie, with three Ju 87s, like first. 1.5 tons. Bombs near the eastern part of the bridgehead. Enemy anti-aircraft defense.
Aug 10, 1938	J/88. With Bf 109s	Escort for K/88, Ju 87s and A. in four sorties.
Aug 10, 1938	Ju 87s	First sortie, with three Ju 87s, against concentrations at Corbera. 1.5 tons. Bombs on the village. Fires. Second sortie, with three Ju 87s, against little bridge to the west of Ginestar. 1.5 tons. Two bombs on bridgehead, on the eastern part. Fire observed. One bomb failed to explode near target.
Aug 11, 1938	J/88. With Bf 109s	Escort for bomber sections, Ju 87s and reconnaissance flight, in two sorties.
Aug 11, 1938	Ju 87s	First sortie, with three Ju 87s, against reserves at Miravet. 1.5 tons. Two bombs on target. One missed target. Second sortie, with three Ju 87s, against little bridge to the west of Ginestar. 1 ton. One bomb on the road, on the east side of the river. Enemy anti-aircraft defense.

Chart VIII
Battle of the Ebro (Continued)

August 1938

Date	Unit	Sorties
Aug 12, 1938	J/88 Ju 87s	No sortie.
Aug 13, 1938	J/88. With Bf 109s	Escort for bomber sections and Ju 87s, in four sorties.
Aug 13, 1938	Ju 87s	First sortie, with three Ju 87s, against little bridge to the west of Ginestar. 1.5 tons. Bombs well placed. Little bridge destroyed and carried away by water. Enemy anti-aircraft defense. Second sortie, with three Ju 87s, against the cut bridge to the south of Mora la Nueva. 1.5 tons. Bombs near target. Enemy anti-aircraft defense.
Aug 14, 1938	A/88	Acquisition of a diagram and photos of the results of the bombing raids of the K/88 and Ju 87s.
Aug 14, 1938	J/88. With Bf 109s	Escort for bomber sections, reconnaissance and Ju 87s, in three sorties.
Aug 14, 1938	Ju 87s	With three Ju 87s, sortie against bridge to the northeast of Ginestar. 1.5 tons, on the road leading to the bridge and alternative target due to enemy fighter defense.

Chart VIII
Battle of the Ebro (Continued)

August 1938

Date	Unit	Sorties
Aug 15, 1938	J/88	With Bf 109s, scort for K and Ju 87s, in five sorties.
Aug 15, 1938	Ju 87s	First sortie: With three Ju 87s, against little bridge 2 km west of Ginestar. 1.5 tons. Hit on the western side of the river and to the west of the road near the little bridge. Enemy anti-aircraft defense. Second sortie: With three Ju 87s, against the same target as the first. 1.5 tons. One bomb on the eastern part of the bridge, on the land. Two bombs near target. Enemy anti-aircraft defense. Third sortie: With three Ju 87s, like the first. 1 ton. One bomb direct hit on the little bridge. The little bridge was cut on the western side. Enemy anti-aircraft defense.
Aug 16, 1938	J/88.	With Bf 109s, escort for K and Ju 87s, in three sorties.
Aug 16, 1938	Ju 87s	First sortie: With three Ju 87s, against bridge to the south of Mora la Nueva. 1.5 tons. Two bombs on the road from the west leading to the bridge. One bomb on the eastern side of the river. Enemy anti-aircraft defense. Second sortie: With three Ju 87s, like the first. 1.5 tons. Bombs near target. Enemy anti-aircraft defense. Third sortie: With three Ju 87s, against new bridgehead at Mora la Nueva. One direct hit. Two bombs near target. Bridgehead destroyed.

	CHART VIII	
	BATTLE OF THE EBRO (CONTINUED)	
	AUGUST 1938	
DATE	UNIT	SORTIES
AUG 17, 1938	J/88	With Bf 109s, Escort for K/88 and Ju 87s.
AUG 17, 1938	Ju 87s	First sortie: With three Ju 87s, against bridgehead to the north of Mora la Nueva. 1.5 tons. Bombs near target. Enemy anti-aircraft defense. Second sortie: With three Ju 87s, like the first. 1.5 tons. Bombs near target and on the road leading to the bridge. Enemy anti-aircraft defense.
AUG 18, 1938	J/88	With Bf 109s, escort for K/88 and Ju 87s.
AUG 18, 1938	Ju 87s	With three Ju 87s, against bridgehead at Mora la Nueva. 1.5 tons. Hits could not be observed due to cloud.
AUG 19, 1938	J/88	With Bf 109s, escort for K and Ju 87s, in seven sorties.
AUG 19, 1938	Ju 87s	First sortie: With three Ju 87s, against concentrations of artillery and munitions near Corbera. 1.5 tons. Bombs on target. Explosions observed. Second sortie: With three Ju 87s, like the first. 1.5 tons. Bombs on target. Explosions observed. Third sortie: With three Ju 87s, like the first. Bombs well placed. Fourth sortie: With three Ju 87s, against the intersection near Venta de Camposines. 1.5 tons. Bombs near target. Enemy anti-aircraft defense.

	CHART VIII BATTLE OF THE EBRO (CONTINUED)	
	AUGUST 1938	
DATE	**UNIT**	**SORTIES**
AUG 20, 1938	J/88	With Bf 109s, escort for the Ju 87s.
AUG 20, 1938	Ju 87s	With three Ju 87s, against enemy artillery positions near Corbera. 1.5 tons. Bombs near target.
AUG 21, 1938	J/88	With Bf 109s, escort for K and Ju 87s. Four sorties.
AUG 21, 1938	Ju 87s	First sortie: With two Ju 87s, against the intersection near Venta de Camposines. 1 ton. Bombs near target. Second sortie: With two Ju 87s, like the first. 1 ton. Bombs near target.
AUG 22, 1938	J/88	With Bf 109s, escort for A/88 and Ju 87s. Five sorties.
AUG 22, 1938	Ju 87s	Three sorties, each time with two Ju 87s, against reserves to the southwest of Fatarella. Bombs well placed. Two hits on concentration of trucks.
AUG 23, 1938	J/88	With Bf 109s, escort for K/88, Ju 87s and A/88. Three sorties.
AUG 23, 1938	Ju 87s	First sortie: Against the intersection at Venta de Camposines. 1 ton. Bombs very near target. Second sortie: Against the town of Fatarella. Bombs on target.

CHART VIII		
BATTLE OF THE EBRO (CONTINUED)		
AUGUST 1938		
DATE	**UNIT**	**SORTIES**
AUG 24, 1938	J/88 Ju 87s	No sortie.
AUG 25, 1938	J/88	Sorties with the Bf 109s, Escort for K/88, the Ju 87s and A/88.
AUG 25, 1938	Ju 87s	One sortie with three aircraft, against assault bridges to the N.W. of Benifallet. 1.5 tons. Bombs very near target and on the road from Benifallet. Enemy anti-aircraft defense.

CHART VIII
BATTLE OF THE EBRO (CONTINUED)

AUGUST 1938

DATE	UNIT	SORTIES
AUG 26, 1938	J/88	First sortie: With three Ju 87s, against reserves at Miravet. 1.5 tons. Good bomb placement. Hits on targets. Enemy anti-aircraft defense. Second sortie: With two Ju 87s, against bridge to the northeast of Ginestar. 1 ton. Bridge more severely cut. Enemy anti-aircraft defense.
AUG 27, 1938	J/88 Ju 87s	Due to the weather, no sortie.
AUG 28, 1938	J/88	With Bf 109s, escort for K/88, Ju 87s and A/88, in two sorties.
AUG 28, 1938	Ju 87s	First sortie: With three Ju 87s, against reserves at Benisanet. 1.5 tons. Two bombs on target, one missed. Enemy anti-aircraft defense. Second sortie: With three Ju 87s, against reserves at Miravet. Two bombs on target, one missed. Enemy anti-aircraft defense
AUG 29, 1938	J/88	No sortie.
AUG 29, 1938	Ju 87s	With three Ju 87s, sorties against reserves at Pinell. Two bombs on target.
AUG 30, 1938	J/88	Due to the weather, no sortie.

	CHART VIII	
	BATTLE OF THE EBRO (CONTINUED)	
	SEPTEMBER 1938	
DATE	**AIRCRAFT**	**SORTIES**
SEP 06, 1938	J/88	With Bf 109s, protection of He 111s, Ju 87s and Do 17s.
SEP 06, 1938	Ju 87s	First sortie: With two aircraft, against the intersection at Venta de Camposines. One bomb on the road, another very close. Second sortie: Two aircraft bombed enemy reserves to the N. of Pinell. Bombs on target.
SEP 07, 1938	J/88	With Bf 109s, protection of He 111s, Ju 87s and Do 17s.
SEP 07, 1938	Ju 87s	One sortie, two aircraft bombed enemy reserve positions to the S.W. of Fatarella. Hits on target.
SEP 08, 1938	J/88 Ju 87s	No sortie, due to bad weather.
SEP 09, 1938	Ju 88	With Bf 109s, protection of He 111s and Ju 87s.
SEP 09, 1938	Ju 87s	One sortie, with three aircraft, against two hills two km to the S. of Fatarella. Hits on target. Defended by anti-aircraft fire.
SEP 10, 1938	J/88 Ju 87s	No sortie, due to bad weather.
SEP 03, 1938	J/88	Sorties with the Bf 109s, escort for K/88, Ju 87s and the reconnaissance flight.
SEP 03, 1938	Ju 87s	With three Ju 87s, four sorties against batteries near Corbera. Two bombs on part of the targets. One not observed.
SEP 04, 1938	J/88	First sortie: With two Ju 87s, against N.E. exit of Corbera. 1 ton on target. Second sortie: With two Ju 87s, against the intersection at Venta de Camposines. 1 ton. Hit on the road.
SEP 04, 1938	Ju 87s	First sortie: With two Ju 87s, against the exit to the N.E. of Corbera. 1 ton on target. Second sortie: With two Ju 87s, against the intersection at Venta de Camposines. 1 ton. Hit on the road.

CHART VIII		
BATTLE OF THE EBRO (CONTINUED)		
SEPTEMBER 1938		
DATE	**AIRCRAFT**	**SORTIES**
SEP 05, 1938	J/88	With Bf 109s, protection of the K., Ju 87s.
	Ju 87s	One sortie, with two aircraft, against the intersection at Venta de Camposines. I ton. Bombs very near target.
SEP 11, 1938	J/88	With Bf 109s, protection of He 111s and Ju 87s.
SEP 11, 1938	Ju 87s	Three aircraft bombed enemy positions to the S. of Fatarella.
SEP 12, 1938	J/88 Ju 87s	No sortie.
SEP 13, 1938	J/88	With Bf 109s, protection of He 111s and Ju 87s.
SEP 13, 1938	J/88 Ju 87s	First sorties. Three aircraft bombed enemy positions to the S.W. of Fatarella. Two hits on target. Second sortie: Three aircraft made a bombing raid as in the first sortie: Bombs on target.
SEP 14, 1938	Ju 88	Another escort sortie protecting the Ju 87s.
SEP 14, 1938	Ju 87s	Two aircraft bombed a train between Paitrosos and Tortosa. Direct hit on the locomotive.
From SEP 15, 1938 To SEP 17, 1938	J/88 Ju 87s	No sortie.
SEP 18, 1938	J./88	Escort for He 111s and Ju 87s.
SEP 18, 1938	Ju 87s	One sortie against reserves at the town of Fatarella. Hits on target.

CHART VIII
BATTLE OF THE EBRO (CONTINUED)

SEPTEMBER 1938

DATE	AIRCRAFT	SORTIES
SEP 20, 1938	J/88	Protection for He 111s, Do 17s and Ju 87s.
SEP 20, 1938	Ju 87s	Three aircraft bombed, in two sorties, the ammunition dump at Paitrosos. Explosion.
SEP 21, 1938	J/88	Protection for Ju 87s and Do 17s.
SEP 21, 1938	Ju 87s	First sortie: Three aircraft made a bombing raid against the ammunition dump at Paitrosos. Second sortie, the same.
SEP 21, 1938	A/88	Second and third sorties: Reconnaissance of the effects of the bombing by the Ju 87s.
SEP 22, 1938	Ju 88	Escort for He 111s, Do 17s and Ju 87s.
SEP 22, 1938	Ju 87s	First sortie, with two aircraft against the station at Ampolla. Second sortie, the same.
SEP 22, 1938	A/88	Reconnaissance of the effects of the bombing by the He 111s and Ju 87s.
SEP 23, 1938	J/88	Protection for He 111s, Ju 87s and Do 17s.
SEP 23, 1938	Ju 87s	One sortie, with three aircraft, against artillery positions to the S.W. of Venta de Camposines.
SEP 23, 1938	A/88	Reconnaissance of the effects of the bombing by the He 111s and Ju 87s.

CHART VIII
BATTLE OF THE EBRO (CONTINUED)

	SEPTEMBER 1938	
DATE	**AIRCRAFT**	**SORTIES**
SEP 24, 1938	J/88	Protection for He 111s, Ju 87s and Do 17s.
SEP 24, 1938	Ju 87s	One sortie, with two aircraft, against artillery positions to the S.W. of Venta de Camposines.
SEP 24, 1938	A/88	Reconnaissance of the effects of the bombing by the He 111s and Ju 87s.
From SEP 25, 1938 to SEP 30, 1938	J/88 Ju 87s	No sortie due to bad weather.

Sequence of the work performed by mechanics on the engine of one of the *Stukas* of 5.J/88.

CHART VIII

BATTLE OF THE EBRO (CONTINUED)

OCTOBER 1938

DATE	UNIT	SORTIES
OCT 01-10, 1938	Ju 88	Two sorties escorting He 111s and Ju 87s.
OCT 01-10, 1938	Ju 87s	Two bombing sorties against enemy positions to the S. of Venta de Camposines.
OCT 02-10, 1938	Ju 88	With Bf 109s, Escort for K/88 and Ju 87s.
OCT 02-10, 1938	Ju 87s	First sortie: With two Ju 87s, first sortie as K. (enemy positions to the southeast of Venta de Camposines. Direct hit on positions.)
OCT 02-10, 1938	A/88	Photographic reconnaissance of the effects of the bombing by K/88 and Ju 87s.
OCT 03-10, 1938	J./88 Ju 87	Escort for He 111s and Ju 87s
OCT 03-10, 1938	Ju 88	First sortie: Two aircraft bombed enemy positions to the S. of Venta de Camposines. Second sortie Two aircraft made a bombing raid against enemy concentrations to the N. of Venta de Camposines.
OCT 03-10, 1938	Ju 87	Reconnaissance of the effects of the bombing by the He 111s and Ju 87s.
OCT 04-10, 1938	J/88	Escort for the He 111s, Ju 87s and Do 17s. Second sortie the same.
OCT 04-10, 1938	Ju 87s	Two aircraft bombed enemy positions to the S. of Venta de Camposines.
OCT 05-10, 1938	J/88 Ju 87s	In the coming days no sorties will be made with the Ju 87s because they have to be overhauled.

No.	Type	Code
1	Ju 87V-4	23-1
2	Ju 87A	29-2
3	Ju 87A	29-3
4	Ju 87A	29-4
5	Ju 87A	29-5
-	-	29-6 (never existed)
6	Ju 87B	29-7
7	Ju 87B	29-8
8	Ju 87B	29-9
9	Ju 87B	29-10
10	Ju 87B	29-11
11	Ju 87B	29-12
12	Ju 87B	29-13

CHART IX
CODES OF JUNKERS JU 87s OPERATING IN SPAIN

The *Stuka Kette "Jolanthe"* served in Spain from February to October 1938 with magnificent results.

CHAPTER 4

Junkers Ju 87 B *Stuka*

Stukas in the K/88 Group

The series-B Junkers Ju 87 *Stukas* arrived in Spain late in 1938 and made their operational debut during the Catalonian campaign.

Once the new Junkers Ju 87B-1 dive-bomber had gone into production for Luftwaffe units, the German high command decided to try out these aircraft in the skies over Spain.

Thus, in October 1938 six new Junkers Ju 87B-1 aircraft were sent to Spain and assembled at the Leon Air Force Depot. These aircraft were allocated numbers 29-7 through 29-12, with one aircraft held in reserve. After the arrival of the 87Bs, the A series aircraft were shipped back to Germany.

The unit was designated as Stuka/K.88 and was commanded by *Oberleutnant* Fritz Glanser. It was made up of thirty-three German air and ground crew, including five pilots, three radio operators, nine mechanics, six armorers, one aircraft engine specialist, two radio technicians, an electrician, four drivers, an interpreter and two clerks. Most of them (twenty-three in total, including all the pilots and radio operators) came from the same unit, the *IV (St.)/LG1* (IV *Stuka* Group of Instruction Wing No.1) based at the aerodrome at Barth, Germany). The new unit was initially stationed at the airfield at Sanjurjo, near Saragossa, together with the twin-engined Heinkel He 111s.

CHART X
DEPLOYMENT OF THE JUNKERS JU 87 "STUKAS" OF THE CONDOR LEGION
DURING THE CATALONIAN OFFENSIVE

DATE	AERODROME	No. OF AIRWORTHY AIRCRAFT
DECEMBER 1938		
DEC 17, 1938	Levante Air Region. La Cenia	4 Ju 87s (29)
DEC 23, 1938	Levante Air Region. La Cenia	4 Ju 87s (29)
DEC 30, 1938	Levante Air Region. La Cenia	1 Ju 87 (29) transferred from Saragossa to Burgos
DEC 31, 1938	North Air Region Leon	1 Ju 87 (29)
DEC 31, 1938	Levante Air Region La Cenia	3 Ju 87s (29)
JANUARY 1939		
JAN 06, 1939	North Air Region. Leon	1 Ju 87 (29)
JAN 06, 1939	Levante Air Region La Cenia	3 Ju 87s (29)
JAN 07, 1939	Levante Air Region. Sanjurjo (Saragossa)	4 Ju 87s (29) transferred from La Cenia to Sanjurjo (Saragossa)
JAN 08, 1939	Levante Air Region Sanjurjo (Saragossa)	1 Ju 87 (29) transferred from Sanjurjo (Saragossa) to X.

CHART X

DEPLOYMENT OF THE JUNKERS JU 87 "STUKAS" OF THE CONDOR LEGION DURING THE CATALONIAN OFFENSIVE (CONTINUED)

	JANUARY 1939	
DATE	AERODROME	NO. OF AIRWORTHY AIRCRAFT
JAN 09, 1939	Levante Air Region. Sanjurjo (Saragossa)	3 Ju 87s (29)
JAN 12, 1939	Levante Air Region Sanjurjo (Saragossa)	4 Ju 87s (29)
JAN 17, 1939	Levante Air Region Sanjurjo (Saragossa)	1 Ju 87s (29) transferred from La Cenia to Sanjurjo (Saragossa)
JAN 22, 1939	Levante Air Region Puig Moreno	3 Ju 87s (29)
JAN 26, 1939 JAN 27, 1939	Levante Air Region La Cenia	12 Bf 109s (6)
	Buñuel	1 He 70 (14) 6 Do 17s (27)
	Tauste	3 He 45s (15) 1 He 70 (14) 3 Do 17s (27)
	Sanjurjo (Saragossa)	21 He 111s (25)
		No Ju 87s appear (29)
JAN 04, 1939	Levante Air Region. Valls	3 Ju 87s (29)

Stuka/K.88 of the Legion Condor entered into operation in the skies over Catalonia on December 22, 1938, after being transferred to the airfield at La Cenia, like their predecessors. That day the Ju 87Bs made eleven take-offs in total, in four sorties, dive-bombing the station and munitions factory at Paitrosos, scoring hits on the station and on a warehouse.

The first six Ju 87s were coded 29-7 through 29-12. Strangely, code 29-6 was missed out and was never assigned.

The Catalonian Campaign

December 23 saw the start of the Catalonian offensive, and the new *Stukas* bombed enemy concentrations at Bobera and Mayals, although during the second sortie the three aircraft taking part had to turn back due to bad weather. On the 25th, six sorties were flown by the Ju 87Bs against Bobera, a concentration of armored vehicles in the Navarre Army Corps sector (in which two bombs scored direct hits on the chosen target), Palma de Ebro, Borjas Blancas and Granadella. In the next three days the targets were Borjas Blancas and Agramunt, hills about 15km to the northeast and southeast of Pobla de Granadella, enemy concentrations at Ulldemolíns and anti-aircraft batteries at Artesa de Segre.

Moving now into January 1939, specifically the 4th, three aircraft made two bombing raids: the first against enemy concentrations at Tarros and the second against the port of Tarragona, where a direct hit was scored against an enemy vessel. On the following days the Ju 87Bs concentrated their attacks on enemy anti-aircraft batteries at Agramunt, scoring direct hits. Dive-bombing raids continued on a practically daily basis, mainly against troop concentrations, communication nodes, road and rail traffic, road and rail bridges and,

The Ju 87Bs carried bombs not only on the belly rack, but also under the wings.

once again, enemy anti-aircraft batteries, scoring a direct hit on one of them on January 12, 1939. On the 7th, Stuka/K.88 was transferred from La Cenia to the airfield at Sanjurjo in Saragossa.

DATE	UNIT	SORTIES
DEC 22, 1938	Ju 87s	Four bombing sorties, in total with eleven aircraft, against station and munitions factory of Paitrosos, scoring hits on the station and on a warehouse.
DEC 23, 1938	Ju 87s	First sortie: Three aircraft bombed concentrations at Bobera and Mayals. Second sortie: Could not be completed due to bad weather. Third sortie: Three aircraft bombed concentrations at Mayals.
DEC 25, 1938	Ju 87s	First sortie: Three aircraft bombed Bobera. Second sortie Three aircraft bombed a concentration of armored vehicles in the Navarre Army Corps sectors, with two direct hits on the target. Third sortie: Three aircraft against the same target. One hit. Fourth sortie: Three aircraft against La Palma de Ebro. Fifth sortie: Three aircraft against Borjas Blancas. Sixth sortie: Three aircraft against Granadella.
DEC 26, 1938	Ju 87s	Two aircraft made two bombing sorties against Borjas Blancas and Agramunt.
DEC 27, 1938	Ju 87s	Four bombing raids against hills some 15 km to the N.E. and S.E. of Pobla de Granadella.
DEC 29, 1938	Ju 87s	Three bombing raids, with a total of six aircraft, against enemy concentrations at Ulldemolíns and enemy flak batteries at Artesa de Segre.

The First Losses

On January 15, the *Stukas* made, among others, two sorties against the port of Tarragona, in which they succeeded in hitting a vessel in the first sortie before sinking it in the second.

The Ju 87Bs did not fly any more sorties until the 21st when they dive-bombed the port of Barcelona with three aircraft. The *Stukas* were attacked by Polikarpov I-15 "Chato" biplanes, of the 4th Squadron of Group No.26 of the Republican Air Force. *Sargento* Francisco Alférez Jiménez, who was flying the aircraft coded CA-029, succeeded in shooting down one of the Ju 87Bs, coded 29-8, which had to make a forced landing near Villanueva y Geltrú, with the crew unhurt. The aircraft actually landed on the beach at Comarruga. Republican dispatches also mention the shooting down of a second Ju 87B, reporting that it crashed into the sea, but there is no record of this second incident.

On the following day the Ju 87s' target was San Sadurní de Noya, and on the 23rd they dive-bombed the bridge located to the west of Martorell.

On January 24, Stuka/K.88 squadron suffered its first blooding. The unit made two sorties to attack the bridge to the southwest of Molíns del Rey: on the second, the aircraft numbered 29-10, crewed by Squadron Leader *Oberleutnant* Fritz Glanser and an *Oberfeldwebel* acting as an observer, was shot down by enemy anti-aircraft fire. Despite being hit, the aircraft managed to land behind its own lines, in a vineyard, but both crewmembers were seriously wounded.

Above: The Junkers Ju 87B coded 29-8 was the only aircraft of this type to be shot down by an enemy fighter. It was forced to land on the beach at Comarruga after being hit by the guns of a Polikarpov I-15 CA-029.

Below: Photographic sequence of Junkers Ju 87B coded 29-10 piloted by the leader of *Stuka./K.88*, shot down by enemy anti-aircraft artillery in the vicinity of Molíns del Rey.

		CHART XI
		OPERATIONS LOGS OF THE JUNKERS JU 87B STUKAS
		THE CATALONIAN OFFENSIVE (CONTINUED)
		JANUARY 1939
DATE	UNIT	SORTIES
JAN 04, 1939	K.88 Ju 87s	Three aircraft made two bombing sorties against enemy concentrations at Tarros and the port of Tarragona, scoring a direct hit on a vessel.
JAN 05, 1939	K.88 Ju 87s	Five heavy bombing raids against enemy concentrations at Pons, anti-aircraft batteries in the Sierra del Señor sector, anti-aircraft batteries at Agramunt (scoring a direct hit on one anti-aircraft battery) and troop concentrations at Agramunt.
JAN 06, 1939	K.88 Ju 87s	Two aircraft bombed the same targets as the He 111s. (Enemy positions near Doncell). Two direct hits on the anti-aircraft batteries at Agramunt.
JAN 07, 1939	K.88 Ju 87s	Two aircraft made three sorties with He 111s. (First sortie: Against the identified targets: unable to complete due to low cloud cover. Second sortie: Bombing of enemy positions at km 11 and km 8.5 of the road from Vilanova de Prades to the west. Third sortie: Bombing of enemy positions on hill 352, 1.5 km to the W.S.W. of Maxet.)
JAN 08, 1939	K.88 Ju 87s	Two aircraft made three sorties with He 111s. (First sortie: Bombing raid against enemy positions near Vilanova de Prades. Second sortie: Bombing of roads between Cornudella, Borjas del Campo and Prades, and bombing of a bridge to the S. of Cornudella, hitting a column of trucks.)

DATE	UNIT	SORTIES
JAN 12, 1939	K.88 Ju 87s	... Second sortie: (Five He 111s and three Ju 87s), against enemy positions on both sides of the Montblanch-Lilla road and bridges to the W. of Tarragona. ... Fourth sortie: (Five He 111s and three Ju 87s), against road traffic Montblach-Valls and anti-aircraft batteries; one bomb from the Ju 87s scored a direct hit on a heavy battery. ... Sixth sortie: (Six He 111s and three Ju 87s), against traffic on the from Lilla to Valls and bridges to the W. of Tarragona.
JAN 13, 1939	K.88 Ju 87s	Three aircraft made two bombing raids against the railway bridge to the E. of Morell, scoring two direct hits.
JAN 14, 1939	K.88 Ju 87s	Three aircraft made four bombing sorties against the same targets as the He 111s. (First sortie: Bombing of the level crossing to the E. of Valls and enemy positions near Valls. Also, the railway bridge at Altafalla. Second sortie: Bombing of the traffic between Alcovert and Reus-Tarragona and the railway bridge at Altafalla. Third sortie: Bombing of the road bridge at Tarragona. Fourth sortie: Bombing of the traffic between Reus and Tarragona and the railway bridge to the E. of Morell.)

On January 27, 1939, after *Oberleutnant* Glanser was wounded, command of the Stuka/K/88 passed to *Oberleutnant* Heinz Bohne, who had arrived with his radio operator, *Uffz.* Karl Fitzner, on January 11 of that same month.

On February 4, the *Stukas* advanced to the former Republican airfield at Valls, but they would no longer be needed to fly missions over the Catalonian front.

The Final Offensive

As replacements for the aircraft damaged by enemy action the last of the twelve Junkers Ju 87 to fly in Spanish skies arrived in Spain. This last aircraft was coded 29-13. In March 1939, the K/88 Group was redeployed to operate over the central front, in the operations that came to be known as the Final Offensive.

On March 4, six aircraft, in two sorties, bombed the viaduct on the Salvacañete road, and the following day they attacked another bridge at Villanueva. In the afternoon, during a sortie in the Teruel area, one of the Ju 87Bs, the one coded 29-11, was seriously damaged by enemy anti-aircraft fire and, crossing the lines, was forced to make an emergency landing. On the 7th, the four airworthy *Stukas* attacked enemy positions in the Viver-Segorbe-Sagunto area over the Teruel front.

On March 15, Stuka/K/88 changed its area of operations to the Madrid front and five Junkers Ju 87Bs bombed the railway stations at Collado Mediano, Collado Villalba and Torrelodones. On the 16th a viaduct on the road south of Meco to the southeast of Guadalajara and the crossroads 4km to the northwest of Fuentidueña del Tajo were attacked. On the following day it was the turn of a railway crossing to the northwest of Arganda while on March 18, three Ju 87Bs bombed enemy positions to the west of Quijorna and artillery battery emplacements to the southeast of Titulcia. On March 20, two aircraft bombed a railway crossing to the northwest of Arganda, the road from Las Rozas to El Escorial, and enemy positions in that sector.

Above: The Junkers Ju 87B coded 29-13 was the last to arrive in Spain, sent to cover aircraft lost or rendered unserviceable.

Below: A *Kette* of Ju 87B at the Saragossa aerodrome.

119

Chart XII
The Final Offensive

March 1939

Date	Unit	Sorties
Mar 04, 1939	Ju 87s	Two sorties, with a total of six aircraft, against the road bridge at Salvacañete.
Mar 07, 1939	Ju 87s	Nine sorties, with 33 He 111s and 3 Ju 87s, against railway installations, roads and enemy positions in the Viver, Segorbe, Sagunto sector, and against vessels and the port, and anti-aircraft batteries in the vicinity of Sagunto. Two perfect hits on the vessels. Enemy anti-aircraft defense.
Mar 15, 1939	Ju 87s	Five aircraft bombed the same targets. (Railway stations at Collado Mediano, Collado Villalba and Torrelodones.)
Mar 16, 1939	Ju 87s	Two aircraft bombed the same targets. (Roads and railway lines to the S.W. of Guadalajara, road bridge to the S. of Meco and intersection 4 km to the N.W. of Fuentidueña).
Mar 18, 1939	Ju 87s	Three aircraft made the same sorties. (Enemy positions to the W. of Quijorna and artillery positions to the S.E. of Titulcia.
Mar 20, 1939	Ju 87s	Two aircraft made the same sorties. (Railway crossing to the N.W. of Arganda, Rozas-El Escorial road, and enemy positions to the N.W. of Quijorna and Casa de las Rentillas.

The last sorties flown by *Stukas* in the Spanish Civil war took place on March 27. That day no fewer than thirteen bombing raids were carried out against enemy columns in the vicinity of Arges. All resistance from the Republican forces ceased, and on March 28 the defenders of Madrid surrendered to the Nationalist troops. The war ended officially on April 1, 1939.

Epilogue

All that remains is to add that three Ju 87Bs flew in a celebratory fly-past at the aerodrome at Barajas (Madrid) in May 1939 and that all surviving aircraft, including the damaged ones, were returned to Germany; none remained in service with the new Spanish Air Force. The bill issued by Germany for the twelve Junkers Ju 87 *Stuka* sent to Spain amounted to DM 1,914,808, the equivalent of 6,586,939.38 pts.

The Junkers Ju 87 *Stuka* and the Republican Air Force

The Republican air force soon found out about the presence in Spain of Junkers Ju 87 *Stuka* dive-bombers. In several Information Bulletins of the Office of the Chief of Staff of the Republican Air Force soon began to gather data about these German aircraft, albeit some of it erroneous.

Thus, the front page of Information Bulletin No.11 of the 2nd Staff Section for June 20, 1938, showed a good quality top and side view of the Junkers Ju 87A, detailing the location of the air brakes, ailerons and flaps. Inside it published, oddly enough, a photograph of the prototype Ju 87V-4; precisely the one which had been in Spain in December 1936 and January 1937. The technical characteristics of the aircraft were also described, pointing out, among other things, that:

JUNKERS Ju.-87

"The bomb it carries is, as we say, from 250 to 500 kg; but the squadron stationed at La Cenia, if it is ever in action, will carry a 250 kg bomb only."

The fact is that 5.J/88 squadron had been operating for over four months. The text finished by saying:

"Perhaps it is another of those aircraft that Germany carries out trials on, preceded by a 'scary' reputation and which, after the trials … is offered for sale to 'friendly' countries."

Apart from the aforementioned drawings, the special edition of the bulletin published in December 1938 included an accurate drawing of the *Jolanthe* pig, complete with an explanation that the emblem was painted on the front part of the wheel fairing. It has to be said that this was an impressive display of knowledge, especially since no aircraft had ever crashed in Republican held territory.

This intelligence no doubt came from information provided by German airmen held prisoner by the Republicans. By way of example we publish the statements of two of them. The first was provided by *Oberleutnant* Wolf Fach, shot down by anti-aircraft fire over the Ebro front in a twin-engined Dornier Do 17 on August 5, 1938. As you can see, it is a very detailed statement:

"At La Cenia there are also 17 or 18 Messerschmitt 109, 3 Junkers Ju-87 dive-bombers, one Heinkel-51 and two or three Heinkel-45s. There are also three mock-ups of Messerschmitt 109s and four mock-ups of Heinkel-51s. The leaders of the two Messerschmitt squadrons are Oberleutnant Seiler and Oberleutnant Eiehlerfeld. He thinks there is another squadron at Villafamés but he isn't sure.

The leader of the Junkers Ju-87s is Oberleutnant Haas and that of the Heinkel-45s is Hauptmann Lampersdorf. He has heard that sometimes there are 10 Fiat CR.32s at Castellón.

For [the anti-aircraft defense] of the airfield at La Cenia there are three batteries of four cannons each. One battery of 8.8s, another two of 3.7s and also some 20 mm machine guns."

Another German prisoner, mechanic *Oberfeldwebel* Erich Naumann, was reported as saying the following in Barcelona on August 21, 1938:

"He has also heard about the Junkers Ju-87s, of which there are one or two in Spain, and which are dive-bombers.

When they went with the squadron to bomb the Ebro bridges they saw some of those aircraft from a distance. He didn't see them at La Cenia the day he landed there."

Naumann also referred to the Henschel Hs 123 *Angelito*:

"He knows that in Germany there are also dive-bombers which are Henschel-122s and 123s. They are one and one-and-a-half wing planes [monoplanes and sesquiplanes]."

(He was shown a photo of a Henschel-123 and was asked what the tank slung between the undercarriage legs was and what it was for. He answered that it was a drop tank for fuel for long flights and that it was fitted in that place because the aircraft was very fast and there was no room on the wings. This tank had a device so that when ignited it could be dropped like a bomb).

"This aircraft carries a maximum of two 50 to 75 kg bombs somewhere under the wings."

As we have seen, the German airmen were quite talkative and the Republicans even knew the name of the officer in charge of the Junkers Ju 87 in Spain, *Oberleutnant* Hermann Haas.

Three of the Ju 88B *Stukas* belonging to K.88 in the fly-past held over Saragossa, at the end of the Spanish Civil War.

Meanwhile, shortly after the start of the Battle of the Ebro, specifically August 2, 1938, the Chief of Staff of the Republican Air Force, *Teniente Coronel* Antonio Martin Luna, sent a teletype to the General Commanding the Eastern Region Group of Armies containing the following information:

"Although the following information may not be correct, it is likely to be so, since no enemy air force is operating on any front other than the Ebro front.

German air force. 50 Messerschmitts, 30 Heinkel 111s, **3 Junkers 87s for dive-bombing, carrying a 250/500 kg bomb,** *8 or 10 Do-17s and 9 Heinkel 51s.*

Likely deployment for the Ebro front. (...)
German:
Bombers and Fighters: Saragossa and La Cenia.
Fighter: Calamocha. Bomber: Alfaro. (...)

If we should receive further information about the above we will report it in due course."

Without a doubt, the information was very close to the truth.

To finish we should point out that this copious information about the German dive-bombers was of hardly any use to the personnel manning the Republican observation stations. In none of the other daily dispatches about enemy aircraft action over the fronts is the presence of Junkers Ju 87s mentioned, despite there being a considerable number of them, as we have seen. When the spotters report dive-bombing actions they always identify the aircraft as Italian Breda Ba 65s, which bear very little similarity to *Stukas*.

Very odd indeed.

As for the Republican fighter pilots, as we have already said, only on one occasion were Junkers Ju 87s correctly identified. A very strange state of affairs.

Rear view of a Ju 87B at the La Cenia airfield, next to a number of bombs, ready to be loaded.

DOCUMENTARY SOURCES

HISTORICAL ARCHIVE OF THE SPANISH AIR FORCE (VILLAVICIOSA DE ODÓN)

·   Information bulletins from the aerodromes at Tablada and Cordoba

·   Operational logs of the Legion Condor

·   Information bulletins from the Republican Air Force

MILITARY HISTORICAL SERVICE (AVILA)

·   Nationalist Information and Operational reports from the Nationalist Air Command.

CIVIL WAR ARCHIVE (SALAMANCA)

·   Republican information bulletins from the 2nd Section of the Staff

BUNDESARCHIV (FREIBURG)

·   Operation "Magic Fire". German intervention from July to October 1936.

·   Die deutsche Luftwaffe im spanischen Buergerkrieg. Legion Condor. Karl Drum.

BIBLIOGRAPHY

LA GUERRA DE ESPAÑA DESDE EL AIRE. Jesús Salas Larrazábal. Ariel. 1969

L'AERÒDROM 329. MONTORNÈS DEL VALLÈS I L'AERONÀUTICA EN LA GUERRA CIVIL ESPANYOLA. David Gesalí Barrera. Publicacions de l'Abadia de Montserrat. 2008.

HENSCHEL HS 123 *Angelito*. Lucas Molina Franco. Quirón Ediciones. Valladolid. 2000

L'AERÒDROM DE LA SÉNIA: 1937-39. Heribert García i Esteller. Published by CEIBM and Patronat del Camp d'Aviació de la Sénia. Valladolid. 2008.

LEGION CONDOR. 1936-1939. EINE ILLUSTRIERTE DOKUMENTATION. Karl Ries and Hans Ring. Verlag Dieter Hoffmann. Mainz. 1980

LEGIÓN CÓNDOR. LA HISTORIA OLVIDADA. Lucas Molina Franco and J.M. Manrique. Quirón Ediciones. Valladolid. 2000

LUFTWAFFE JU 87 DIVE-BOMBER UNITS. 1939-1941. Peter C. Smith. Ian Allan Publishing. Surrey. 2006

JUNKERS JU 87 VOL. II. Marek J. Murawski. Kagero. Lublin 2006

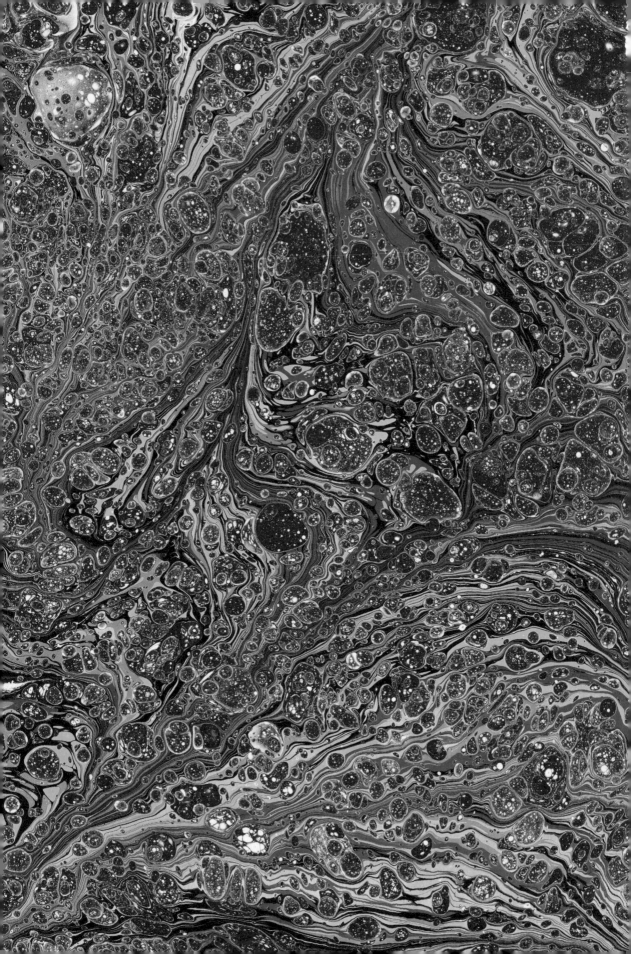